THE LIBERTY KEYS

GOD'S INSTRUCTIONS FOR KEEPING AMERICA FREE

Terry L. Kirby

To the Glory of God
For My Wife
For My Girls
For America

CONTENTS

"Freedom is never more than one generation away from extinction. We didn't pass it to our children with the bloodstream. It must be fought for, protected, and handed on for them to do the same."

President Ronald Reagan
State of the Union Address
January 19, 1985

FOREWORD

In the summer of 2014 my wife and I visited Mount Vernon, the home of George Washington, for the second time. Our first trip had been in the winter of 2000. These two trips could not have been more different. The summer trip was hot and humid, like most of the summers along the Potomac River. The winter trip was cold and hindered by ice and snow. Not only were the weather conditions polar opposites, there had been some drastic changes in our lives. I had a different job and we had moved to a new town. Our two daughters had grown up and were attending college.

Sadly, America had changed even more. The gradual changes that are hardly noticed over time were replaced by accelerated changes on an epic scale. The innocence of the pre-September 11, 2001 world was gone. America was not only the victim of the September 11 attacks, but it was also ground zero for the negative change that followed, a change for the worse. We were moving away from our founding principles and becoming less American. Our freedom was slipping away. The changes started with subtle liberties being removed in our travel. There were longer delays at our airports; the TSA was making air travel a painful experience.

Countless and precious resources were being used to fight the two wars in Iraq and Afghanistan. The housing and automobile industry crashed. The change continued with other parts of our government growing out of control. The politicians responsible for this massive growth of government proclaimed that improvements in national security and economic stability were their only goals. Although interest rates had decreased, taxes increased. The price of everything went up as personal income dropped. Millions of jobs were lost as businesses closed or moved overseas. Many full-time jobs turned into part-time jobs. There was a general shrinking of our once unstoppable economy.

News outlets were calling this "the new normal." The new normal meant that Americans had to settle for their hopes of fulfilling the American Dream, which had been the driving force behind our economy for almost two centuries, being put on hold, scaled back, or even lost. We previously believed that if we wanted to be successful and fulfill our dreams all we had to do was work hard. We believed our children should have a better life than we had lived.

Even though there has been a huge change in leadership of America as a result of the 2016 elections, it is too early to know if the Trump Administration's plans and policies will make significant strides to improve the current conditions we face. The election results have had a ripple effect around the world. As America goes, so goes the rest of the world. Weak economies, political turmoil, and war are the norm for many parts of the world. It is a frightening time to live. For now, no country is safe; no individual is safe.

During my second visit to Mount Vernon I longed to revisit George Washington's estate not only to be reminded of its grandeur but also to revisit the wonders of America's founding. I wanted to see Washington's America again and take my mind off the challenges we face as a country. I must admit that my hope for America's future was reinvigorated while we walked around the grounds of this founding father's estate.

The second part of the tour included a visit to the main house, where everything changed for me. As we entered the house, our tour guide described it in excellent detail. In the central passage our guide reminded us of one particular item in the collection of artifacts there. I suppose I had forgotten about it from my first visit, but there is a small, rectangular box that hangs prominently on the wall in the central passage. This wooden box with a glass front holds what looks like an old, over-sized skeleton key. But this is no ordinary key.

The key that hangs on the wall at Mount Vernon is the key to the main door of the Bastille, the infamous prison in Paris, France. The Bastille had been built in the fourteenth century as part of the defenses of Paris. In the seventeenth century the structure had been converted into a prison to hold the king's political enemies. This prison had gained a well-deserved reputation of brutality and became a symbol of the tyranny of the French monarchy.

In France, the beginnings of a revolution began to take shape in 1789. The people had grown tired of their poverty and near starvation. They began to fight back against the poor leadership of King Louis XVI with a series of rebellious acts that led to the weakening of the king's power and control. One of those acts was led by the general of the national guard in Paris, the Marquis de Lafayette. He ordered the Bastille destroyed. General Lafayette, as a young Frenchman, had volunteered to serve in the Continental Army and became General George Washington's aide-de-camp during the Revolutionary War. These men developed a type of father-son relationship during their service in the Continental Army. After the war, Lafayette returned to France as a national hero, which led to his appointment as the leader of the national guard.

After the Bastille was destroyed, Lafayette wanted Washington to have the main door key and sent it to him on what would be a seven-year journey that ended at Mount Vernon in 1797, just before Washington's second term ended as president of this new nation called the United States of America. Lafayette said in his letter that accompanied this gift that it was "a tribute I owe as a son to my adoptive father, as an aide-de-camp to my general, as a missionary of liberty to its patriarch."[1] The first person Lafayette trusted with the key was Thomas Paine, the author of *Common Sense*. Paine wrote Washington a letter that accompanied the key on May 1, 1790. He expressed the honor that was his to be entrusted with "this early trophy of the Spoils of Despotism and the first ripe fruits of American principles transplanted into Europe to his great Master and Patron."[2] The key was finally presented to Washington in New York by John Rutledge Jr., of South Carolina, who was returning to America from London. The key moved with Washington to Philadelphia when the United States government moved there in the fall of 1790.

As our tour guide continued her description of the central passage and as we continued our tour of the main house, I could not take my mind off that key and the word "liberty." Considering the liberty that America has gained at such an enormous price of lives, fortunes, and sacred honor, I could not accept the reality that my generation of Americans was giving up these same liberties without a fight. Liberty is our birthright. Liberty is America. If we give away our liberty, we cease to be America.

Today America seems to be in a mad dash to give up what should be our most precious national treasure, our liberty. There is a destructive force at work. These forces are trying to take away our freedom and replace it with tyranny. Tyranny is a government structure that places all the power over society in the hands of a single person or very small groups of government officials. These forces are found inside and outside our borders. Inside forces are our own politicians and activists who want power and for America to pay a heavy price for being the lone superpower. They believe that America's ability to become the only superpower was accomplished to the detriment of other peoples and nations. They want America to be damaged or degraded in order to be on equal footing with the rest of the world. Outside forces are those coming into America with no intention of becoming Americans but instead remaining loyal citizens of their home countries. They benefit by living within the borders of America but have no desire to assimilate and legally become citizens of the United States of America. Other outside forces are crossing our borders as hostile fighters who desire to intentionally harm America and Americans. These groups are directed by terrorist groups or even foreign governments. Radio talk show host Rush Limbaugh has described on numerous occasions that this is no longer immigration to America but an invasion of America. Americans are giving up their personal liberties because of the pressures of political correctness, fear, brainwashing from our own media outlets, desire for security, apathy, or a lack of national pride.

My question for my fellow Americans is this: Why do you want to go back into tyranny when your freedom is what sets us apart from the rest of the world? Today we need to live in and even expand our liberties, not give them up for the false argument of "fairness" or "This is not my America." Many Americans are living under the false hope that a series of election victories ensures the return to our founding principles. Our country seems more divided that ever. The opposition to the Trump presidency seems more determined than ever to see that his policies fail. America is just one or two elections cycles away from being back in the mess we are trying to escape. We must remain vigilant.

We are giving our liberty away to a small group of Americans, namely politicians, many who do not have our best interest at heart. We need to re-declare our independence from the tyranny of big government and go back to the strict adherence of our founding principles set out in the Declaration of Independence and the United States Constitution. We need to reestablish the rule of law in America. To survive we must be a nation of laws and law-abiding citizens.

You may be asking yourself, "What can I do about it?" That is a great question. I have asked myself that question many times. That question takes me back to the central passage at Mount Vernon. As I stood there looking at the key to the Bastille while the word "liberty" rang in my ears, I remembered that I stood there as an American. All Americans can make a difference. As I state below, if we all exercise our freedom to vote and participate in the political process we can help secure our freedom for generations to come. My fellow Americans, we can no longer be apathetic if we want to maintain our freedom as Americans.

I also stood there staring at the key as a Christian, a follower of Jesus Christ. I knew that I was not alone in this fight because I knew that my God, the God of the Bible, can do anything. What I am saying is that my God has promised me that he would hear and answer my prayers according to his perfect will. I realized at that moment that not only do Christian Americans have the same freedoms as other Americans to make a difference, but as Christian Americans our God can use his unlimited power when we call upon him to rescue America from tyranny and facilitate our return to our founding principles. I am not suggesting for an instant that God only works in or for America. Also, please do not dismiss the content of my book because of my point of view. But I do believe, with every fiber of my being, that many Christian Americans feel the same way that I do. I believe if all Christian Americans follow my recommendations, America will be freed from this growing tyranny and will return to our founding principles of freedom within the rule of law, the United States Constitution.

Let me define what I mean when I refer to myself as a Christian. As a Christian or Christ follower, I believe that the Lord Jesus Christ is the only way that one can enter into heaven. I believe what the holy Bible says in John 14:6: "Jesus said to him, 'I am the way, and the truth, and the life; no one comes to the Father but through Me.'" I also believe what Romans 10: 9 says: "that if you confess with your mouth Jesus as Lord, and believe in your heart that God raised Him from the dead, you will be saved." As a Christ follower, I also believe that the holy Bible is the only Word of God. 2 Timothy 3:16 states: "All Scripture is inspired by God and profitable for teaching, for reproof, for correction, for training in righteousness."

As I stood staring at that key, I firmly believe that God called and challenged me to write this book to help you answer the question, What can I do to help America return back to our founding principles? In writing this book I am striving to be obedient to God's call on my life to challenge my fellow Christian Americans to act and do their part to help save our country from those who desire to remake it into something that our founders would not recognize. I hope after reading The Liberty Keys that you will be able to answer this question for yourself and be obedient to what God is calling you to do to rescue and preserve our country for future generations. Previous generations of Americans preserved our freedom; let us do the same for the generations that follow us.

Many in our society have been conditioned to believe that the government is the only organization that can provide solutions for our problems. With all of that false hope for governmental solutions goes our freedom that was earned at a great price. My prayer is that Christian Americans using the rule of law as established in the United States Constitution will help reestablish America's proper footing for our long journey to recovery.

Who can better understand the value of liberty than Christian

Americans who have received liberty in two ways? First, as Christ followers we have received the liberty Jesus Christ provided on the cross and through His resurrection. Second, as Americans we have received the liberty that our forefathers provided in our founding documents and with their blood. This precious American blood continues to be shed to maintain our freedom.

I do not claim to be an expert in American history or politics, but I do have a great passion for our history and a love for America. I want America to continue to be great for all future generations. My love and passion for America has even a more personal source. My father was part of the "greatest generation." He was a decorated veteran of World War II who made many sacrifices to help defeat the enemies of liberty. This same story could be told by millions of other veterans or families of veterans who fought and died in this great cause. Our history, their history, cannot be forgotten or dishonored. Our battle to restore freedom for America is worth fighting for many reasons. One reason is the high price paid by our fellow Americans for our freedom. Another is that future generations of Americans must have the opportunity to be free.

Thank you for your investment of time in the reading of this book. It is my humble privilege and great joy to share this with you. I pray that God will receive any glory gained from the impact this work has on our great country. I also pray that God will use Christian Americans to make our country great again by our returning to its founding documents as our guide and rule of law beginning now and continuing for future generations.

INTRODUCTION

The Liberty Keys is a call to action for Christian Americans to help stop America from moving away from the wisdom of our foundational documents and becoming a nation that would be unrecognizable to our founding fathers. Many Christian Americans have been silent much too long. It is time for us to act before this precious gift of God called America is only a memory for some or only a notation in the history books yet to be written. Many Americans have placed their hope in President Donald Trump to make America great again. For America to be truly great again, we the people must act. Why should we care? From a purely patriotic perspective, America is our country and is great because of its founding and the freedoms that were established and are passionately preserved. Why would any sensible citizen be willing to give up their freedom for tyranny?

Many in America today want to move away from our design and create an unmanageable system that drives our country of order into chaos. A growing group of politicians and other influential leaders are aggressively chipping away at our freedom through hidden legislation or by illegal dictates designed to change America's very nature. This group has many names: the political class, the establishment, the ruling Class. Whatever its name, these people are destroying the fabric of America for their own political power and personal gain. The battle is no longer between two political parties; it is now a war between the ruling class and their supporters and the American people who desire their county to remain as founded.

From a Christian perspective, God has used free Christian Americans to do amazing work for his kingdom in America and around the world. In addition, God uses a wealth of American vocational and volunteer missionaries and the countless financial resources of other Christian Americans for the cause of Christ. If our freedoms continue to be taken away, Christ followers in America will not be able to openly share their faith stories with others. If Christian Americans want to remain free to practice their faith and live in freedom, our liberty must be maintained no matter the cost. The question remains, How do we do it?

The Bible Tells Us How to Save America

Not surprisingly, the keys to saving America are clearly spelled out in the Bible. As people of faith, we believe that the Bible is the only absolute truth. We must be willing to do what it says in all matters of our lives. We must also seek its instruction on how to save America. The two liberty keys are found in Galatians 5:1: "It was for freedom that Christ set us free; therefore keep standing firm and do not be subject again to a yoke of slavery." What do those words have to do with saving America? Read it again and slower this time. "It was for freedom that Christ set us free; therefore keep standing firm and do not be subject again to a yoke of slavery." This passage gives us the two keys that can show us how to save America. First, we need to remember that we are free. Second, we need to stand firm our freedom and not return to tyranny. There will be more about this in a moment.

Paul faced a significant challenge in Galatia. He hoped that his divinely inspired letter would fix the growing problem. New believers in Jesus Christ were adding Judaism to their faith in Jesus Christ. More specifically, Christ followers were adding obedience to the Old Testament law to the gift of grace they had received from God by their faith in the fact that God had raised Jesus from the dead. To describe what they did in more contemporary terms, the new Christ followers in Galatia were living free in Jesus Christ, but they were willing to add obedience to Old Testament law as a part of their freedom in Christ. Paul's main argument against this move back into "slavery" is recorded in three verses. Galatians 3: 1–3 states, "You foolish Galatians, who has bewitched you, before whose eyes Jesus Christ was publicly portrayed as crucified? This is the only thing I want to find out from you: did you receive the Spirit by the works of the Law, or by hearing with faith? Are you so foolish? Having begun by the Spirit, are you now being perfected by the flesh?"

Why were they so willing to give up their freedom in Jesus Christ? The answer is simple. A small group of leaders in the church (Judaizers) wanted these new Christ followers to practice Judaism as a part of their adherence to Christianity. These Judaizers intimidated the new Christ followers in the absence of Paul's strong leadership. In Galatians 5:1 Paul reminds his readers about their freedom in Christ and warns them concerning their need to maintain that freedom.

What does this first key point found in Galatians 5:1a, "It was for freedom that Christ set us free . . .," say to every American today? It is simple. We need to remember that we are free. We are free because we declared ourselves to be free from the tyranny of King George III of England on July, 4, 1776. The Declaration of Independence is the document that the founding fathers signed declaring their freedom. After they declared their freedom they had to win it on the battlefields of the Revolutionary War. We need to revisit the words of this great masterpiece to remind ourselves that we are free and should fight against any movement that strives to take our freedom away. The first liberty key found in Galatians 5:1a connects us to the Declaration of Independence and reminds us that we are free.

What does the second key found in Galatians 5:1b, ". . . therefore keep standing firm and do not be subject again to a yoke of slavery," say to every Americans today? These words serve as a warning for us to stand firm in our freedom and not being subject again to tyranny. The first part of this warning is "keep standing firm." How do we stand firm in our freedom? Each citizen, future citizen, or guest in our country must obey the rule of law, which is the United States Constitution. This document as amended is the design or framework of our freedom. We need to stand firm in on our design because it is the foundation of our identity as Americans. Politicians and ordinary citizens need to live by our rule of law. The second liberty key found in Galatians 5:1b connects us to the United States Constitution and should remind us that we are designed to stand firm in our freedom by keeping our laws.

The second part of this warning is, "do not be subject again to a yoke of slavery." How do we prevent ourselves from being subject again to a yoke of slavery? This slavery is not blatant and visible like the human slavery that plagues our history. This slavery is hidden. It is seen in the disappointment of unfulfilled dreams, the exhaustion of working harder for less, and an overwhelming feeling of helplessness. This slavery is seen in the removal of personal freedoms through higher taxes, increased government regulations, and the government's takeover of sectors of society such as healthcare.

Galatians 5:1b warns us not to fall back into the situation that our founders fought to escape. With the enslavement efforts of an ever-growing federal government, ordinary citizens can respond in one of two ways. We can either accept it as a means to an acceptable end, which is a perverted sense of security in the hands of an all-powerful government. We slip back into tyranny as a country when free citizens are willing to allow the lawless actions of our leaders to continue. Instead, we must hold these law-breaking leaders accountable as, "we the people." We must stand firm in our freedom.

For those of us who desire America to remain as founded, there is a distressing willingness on the part of our fellow Americans to allow this shift back to our oppressive past that was commonplace prior to our founding. If we would just inform ourselves of the days and conditions prior to our founding, we would see the warning signs. We must educate ourselves in American history in order to see this shift back in time. King George III of England headed the centralized tyrannical government of England that oppressed the colonies in America. The colonies were being unreasonably taxed by England without being represented in the English Parliament. The people longed to be free from England and therefore set into motion a process to accomplish this goal. Our founders paid a heavy price to earn and maintain America's freedom. Today, many Americans and those living in America are freely giving up their liberty because they have not had to pay a price to defend it from those forces desiring to take it away. The freedoms designed by our founders are slipping away without a fight or a shot being fired. I pray that the Trump administration will do its part in returning America back to our founding principles, but remember, the job is ours as "we the people."

Important History Lessons in *The Liberty Keys*

Do you want examples outside of the Bible? Remember Lafayette's gift to George Washington? It was a simple key to the main door of the Bastille. It is a powerful symbol of the dangers of tyranny. Lafayette's France attempted to throw off the shackles of tyranny but failed, and they soon returned to their bondage under a new leader named Napoleon. After a tremendous price was paid, France's revolution failed. They did not stand firm in their freedom.

Although the price was high, the American Revolution was successful. The United States of America was built upon the United States Constitution. Succeeding generations of Americans enjoy the benefits of our founder's legacy. *The Liberty Keys* will compare and contrast America and France before, during, and after their revolutions. The primary lesson of this study is that America stood and continues to stand in freedom, but France did not. For America to remain free we must stand firm on the founding principles found in the Declaration of Independence and the United States Constitution.

Liberty Key 1 We Are Free!

The Declaration of Independence was the Second Continental Congress's statement to the world that said, "America is free from all political, economic and military shackles of Great Britain." This was the point-of-no-return moment for the founders. They declared their freedom from England before they won it. If the war that was already raging had ended in failure, the signers of the Declaration of Independence would have been treated as traitors and punished accordingly.

The freedoms we enjoy in America are historic and unique. At no time in world history has there been a nation designed for its people to be free. When our founders declared their freedom from England, they stated in the Declaration of Independence these immortal words, "We hold these truths to be self-evident, that all men are created equal, that they are endowed by their Creator with certain unalienable Rights, that among these are Life, Liberty and the pursuit of Happiness."

The first liberty key in *The Liberty Keys* includes four chapters. Chapter 1 looks at the freedom desired by the American colonies and France. Chapter 2 reviews the freedom declared by both the colonies and France and includes the full text of the Declaration of Independence and the Declaration of the Rights of Man and Citizen of France. Chapter 3 is a study of freedom defined that reveals the fact that Jesus Christ is the only source of true freedom for all people. Finally, chapter 4 records freedom's demise in France immediately following their revolution and the demise of freedom in the United States of America today.

Liberty Key 2
We Must Stand Firm in Our Freedom!

Liberty needs structure. The United States Constitution is the structure of America's freedom. The goal of the Constitution is to protect the rights of the citizens of the United States of America. Each time the Constitution is ignored or openly broken by an ordinary citizen or even the president, our freedom is diminished. The founders designed America to properly function only when the Constitution is followed. Any attempt to undermine or change the Constitution in ways that are not prescribed in the document itself is un-constitutional. Liberty key 2 reminds Americans that it is vitally important that we continue to follow the Constitution as written and signed by the founders and approved by the states if we want to remain free. It is damaging to the very foundation and fiber of this great country for the United States Constitution to be disregarded. This type of behavior cannot be accepted.

The second liberty key in *The Liberty Keys* also includes four chapters. Chapter 5 looks at freedom's design, a biblical model. In this chapter we will look at Romans 13:1-7 and see what the Bible says about how citizens are to interact with their government. It is critically important to understand what the Bible says about how Christ followers are to live under the authority of the government. Chapter 6 reviews the American model of freedom's design. This chapter includes a full copy of the United States Constitution. Chapter 7 will show five ways Americans can stand firm in freedom. Finally, chapter 8 will share five ways Americans who are Christ Followers can uniquely stand firm in freedom.

The Liberty Keys is a book of hope. It is a hope for America to remain strong. It is a hope that Americans can live their dreams in peace. It is a hope that future generations of Americans will remain free. As Christian Americans, may God grant us success as we do our part to help save America! To God be the glory for great things he will do!

LIBERTY KEY 1

We Are Free!

CHAPTER 1
Freedom Desired

Without taking a long and exhausting journey through the history of the world, it would not be an exaggeration to say that a new nation designed for its citizens to live in freedom would be extraordinary. If that same nation's government had as its purpose to "establish justice, insure domestic tranquility, provide for the common defense, promote the general welfare and secure the blessings of liberty to ourselves and our posterity," that would also be extraordinary. Societal freedom was non-existent in nations and kingdoms because citizens, subjects, and slaves have been used to defend or provide the wealth for their kings and rulers throughout recorded history. When leaders declared their sovereignty or absolute authority, their people's limited rights became even more restricted. These leaders controlled their subjects through intimidation; they controlled the supply of the necessities of life and had the ultimate power over life and death.

It defies logic that leaders would freely give away their power and put it into their people's hands. They would not. History has proven this to be the case. So how can citizens gain freedom? The ideal way is to start from the establishment of a new nation. This would explain why freedom is so rare. Freedom or liberty has to be the foundation of a country's design and reflected in its structure. The design has to be developed in such a way that it will be maintained even as leaders and generations come and go.

Thus, the story of America is exceptional in world history. After a series of hostile acts by the king of England, the colonies declared their freedom from his tyranny. France was also a country controlled by a powerful king. The French people also wanted to be free from the tyranny of a powerful king. Let us look at the stories of the Colonialists in America and people of France and how they both desired freedom.

The Colonies

The Colonialists Wanted Freedom

When the first group of Europeans landed on the shores of North America, no one knew that this wilderness would become the land of the free. Even from its beginnings, the colonies were a place where many of its inhabitants were independent and self-reliant. They may have felt this way because of the vastness of the ocean that separated America from Europe or because of the rugged nature of the North American continent. The people felt free to live their lives and practice their religion with limited government interference. The Puritans are an example of a religious group that moved to North America. The Puritans did not want to be a part of the Church of England and were forced to go to a land where they were free to live, work, and worship. Over time, thousands of people made the dangerous trip across the Atlantic Ocean from Europe, looking to have a fresh start in life or to begin the search for riches.

As time passed and the colonies grew and prospered, the British government began to take notice. When governments or kingdoms need money, they historically take it by force from their own citizens. England had a huge debt as a result of the French and Indian War. England needed new sources of revenue, so it turned its attention to its colonies. Parliament was taxing its British citizens in the colonies without representation in Parliament back in England. "No taxation without representation" became a rallying cry for the American colonies. In his book, *A Citizen's Introduction to the Declaration of Independence and the Constitution*, Matthew Spalding states, "The American Revolution began as a tax revolt."[1] The colonialists were not going to remain silent or passive much longer.

Below is a list of events and actions that continued to build resentment between the colonialists and the king of England. This resentment would later turn into hostility that ultimately resulted in the signing of the Declaration of Independence.

March 22, 1765—Stamp Act

This was the first tax directly imposed on the colonies from the British Parliament on transactions occurring within the colonies. This was a levy on just about every type of legal document. Examples include marriage licenses, college degrees, newspapers, and playing cards. This stamp was not like a modern-day postage stamp that would be affixed to the document. It was more like an impression put on to the document. As a result of this tax, the colonists began to boycott British products. Because of the negative response and violence caused by the Stamp Act, the British Parliament repealed it in 1766.

June 29, 1767—Townshend Act

This act passed by the British Parliament placed taxes on glass, lead, paint, paper, and tea. England sent four thousand troops to stop the protests that resulted from these new taxes. In 1770 the British Parliament repealed all the Townshend taxes except the tax on tea.

March 5, 1770—Boston Massacre

A group of British soldiers, who had been sent to Boston to maintain peace during the unrest because of the Townshend Act were surrounded by an unfriendly crowd. The soldiers opened fire, killing three colonists and wounding two others. The soldiers were tried for murder but were only convicted of lesser crimes.

April 27, 1773—Tea Act

British Parliament passed the Tea Act. This reduced the tax on imported British tea. This gave British merchants an advantage when selling their tea in the colonies.

December 16, 1773— Boston Tea Party

A group of 116 men disguised as Indians boarded British ships and dumped 90,000 pounds of tea in Boston Harbor.

September 5–October 26, 1774—First Continental Congress

This First Continental Congress met in Philadelphia. Twelve of the thirteen colonies sent fifty-six delegates. The only colony that did not participate was Georgia. Much of the debate centered on what would be called the Declaration of Rights. This declaration affirmed the body's loyalty to King George III but disputed Parliament's right to tax the colonies. After this action was taken, the First Continental Congress was dismissed.

March 23, 1775—The Speech of Patrick Henry

Patrick Henry gave his famous speech, "Give me liberty or give me death" on this date at St. John's Church in Richmond, Virginia. The speech was made during the third Virginia Convention to discuss relations between the colonies and Great Britain.

April 19, 1775—The Revolutionary War Begins

The Revolutionary War began with the Battles of Lexington and Concord on April 19, 1775. The war lasted for eight years and finally ended with the signing of the Treaty of Paris on September 3, 1783.

May 10, 1775–1781—Second Continental Congress

This Second Continental Congress met in Philadelphia, Pennsylvania. At this point the Revolutionary War had already started with the Battles of Lexington and Concord. One of the first acts of this congress was to establish the Continental Army. On June 15, 1775, Congress appointed George Washington as commander-in-chief of the Continental Army. At the end of September 1777, the Congress had to move out of Philadelphia because British troops occupied the city. This congress continued its work in York, Pennsylvania.

July 8, 1775—Olive Branch Petition

The Second Continental Congress adopted a petition written by John Dickinson declaring its loyalty to King George III. On August 23, 1775, King George III rejected this request and declared that the colonies were in rebellion.

January 9, 1776—Common Sense

A pamphlet entitled "Common Sense" written by Thomas Paine was first published. Paine spoke out against the monarchical form of government. Within six months over 500,000 copies were sold. This pamphlet contains the quote, "These are the times that try men's souls." Paine's work increased the cry for independence from the rule of King George III.

The French

The French Wanted Freedom

The French, with their men and money, played a vital role in America's winning of the American Revolution. The freedom that the Americans gained from England appealed to the French as they faced their own brewing crisis back home with King Louis XVI. The French were living under the control of an inept king who had mismanaged French resources, leading to the citizens' near starvation and poverty. Many of the returning Frenchmen, who had served as officers in the Continental Army, hungered for the taste of freedom that their fight in America had created. James Gains notes in his book, *For Liberty and Glory*, "Lafayette, like many of the French soldiers and officers, took back to France a less nuanced, entirely enthusiastic vision of the American Revolution, the story of a great-hearted people's triumph over despotic power in the cause of their inalienable human rights, the creation of a new society based on equality and civil liberty."[2]

Below is a list of events that led to increased resentment against the French Monarchy and that ultimately led to its fall.

May 10, 1774—King Louis XVI became King of France

Louis Auguste was born on August 23, 1754, and crowned Louis XVI, King of France, after the death of his father, King Louis XV. King Louis XVI possessed few of the same organizational, political, and leadership skills of his father. Louis XVI preferred living the privileged life at Versailles rather than managing the affairs of his kingdom.

February 1787—Assembly of Notables

The French economy was in the middle of a major crisis in the 1780s. The reasons for the crisis were many. The two main reasons were the costs of the wars fought in Europe and funded in America and the low yielding crop harvests. The result of this crisis was a country of mainly poor, hungry, and angry citizens who were upset at King Louis XVI and his leadership. The king turned to his finance minister, Charles de Calonne, for the solution. His solution was to call representatives of the French nobles together and tell them that they would be taxed on their land holdings. The Assembly of Notables was not pleased with this solution and rejected it. No solution was reached and the crisis continued to grow.

June 7, 1788—The Day of the Tiles

The town of Grenoble was the location of the first bloodshed of the French Revolution. The French people had grown tired of the laws restricting their lives for the benefit of the king and his officials. A group of city workers were protesting these oppressive laws, and the Parlement of Dauphiné declared the royal laws illegal. Protesters bombarded the soldiers, sent to break up the protest, with roof tiles.

January 1789—"What is the Third Estate?"

Emmanuel Sieyès' pamphlet, "What is the Third Estate?" was published.
In France there were three orders of citizens. The first estate was the nobility. The second estate was the clergy. The Third Estate was everyone else. A

huge concern was that the first two estates were exempt from paying any taxes, so the entire tax burden fell upon the Third Estate. This pamphlet, which denounced the nobility, became the battle cry of the third estate.

May 5, 1789—Convening of the Estates General

King Louis XVI's next action in his effort to end the financial crisis in France was to convene the Estates General. This was the first time the Estates General had been convened in 160 years. Susan Dunn in her book, *Sister Revolutions: French Lightning, American Light*, states, "Louis felt he had no choice but to convene the Estates General, a kind of National Assembly comprising elected representatives of the three orders of France– the nobility, the clergy, and the 'Third Estate,' composed of all the other inhabitants of France. The king's advisers hoped that somehow the Estates General would help resolve the desperate crisis."[3] Dunn continues, "No one knew what should be the number of deputies, the relationship among the orders, the mode of election, or the procedure for deliberation. Only Louis had the authority to say what the guidelines would be, but the hapless, ineffective monarch said nothing."[4] Dunn finally expresses the hopes of this historic meeting and states, "Everyone awaited the momentous meeting of the Estates General, hoping that this body could restore financial order as well as address burning questions of liberty and equality."[5] No immediate solution was reached and the crisis continued to grow.

June 17, 1789—Creation of the French National Assembly

The French National Assembly was formed out of the Estates General, made up exclusively of members of the third estate. The third estate made up 97 percent of the French population. The polity of the Estates General gave representatives of each of the three estates only one vote. This made it impossible for the Third Estate to ever be in the majority. Because they were always in the minority and their voices were never heard, they formed their own governmental body called the French National Assembly.

Dunn states in *Sister Revolutions* that "The French National Assembly became a monster that destroyed the Revolution, not because it consisted of only one chamber, but because it swallowed up all the other branches of government, permitting on independent judiciary and creating no legitimate place for dissent and opposition."[6]

June 20, 1789—The Tennis Court Oath

As a result of the creation of the French National Assemble, King Louis XVI locked out the representatives of the third estate from the meeting of Estates General. Because of this, the National Assembly met on an indoor tennis court, *Jeu de Paume*, at Versailles, France. At this meeting the Tennis Court Oath was established. It stated that the National Assembly would not disband until they had drawn up a national constitution for France. This was the first act of rebellion against Louis XVI.

The Story Continues

The step from a desire for freedom to an action that results in freedom is a gigantic and risky one. Politically talented, brave, and bold colonialists came together to take action concerning their desire to separate the colonies from the tyranny of King George III. If their actions failed, their heroic efforts would be in vain and they would pay the ultimate price for their treason.

The third estate of France was in a battle for survival. Because of King Louis XVI's leadership and the worsening conditions in France, drastic action was required to improve and even save their lives. Their actions would take down a monarchy and lead to the death of thousands of their fellow citizens.

The next chapter tells the story of how the colonies and the French took this giant step to declare their freedom.

CHAPTER 2
Freedom Declared

The Colonies

The founders would pass the point of no return when the Second Continental Congress met in Philadelphia to approve and sign the Declaration of Independence. The events surrounding the signing of this document would forever change the history of the world.

The Colonies Declared Their Freedom

July 2, 1776—Adoption of the Declaration of Independence

The Second Continental Congress, assembled in Philadelphia, formally adopted the recommendation of Richard Henry Lee's resolution for a Declaration of Independence to break ties with Great Britain. This resolution was made on June 7, 1776. A committee of five men was selected to draft a copy of this declaration, whose primary author was Thomas Jefferson. This declaration allowed America to seek support and alliances from other countries. The primary country that assisted America was France.

July 4, 1776—Final Approval and Signing of the Declaration of Independence

America's independence from Great Britain became official when the final version of the Declaration of Independence was approved on July 4, 1776. Too many Americans have never read this incredible document. It is time to change this sad fact. Enjoy reading it for the first time or the next time.

Declaration of Independence

When in the Course of human events, it becomes necessary for one people to dissolve the political bands which have connected them with another, and to assume among the powers of the earth, the separate and equal station to which the Laws of Nature and of Nature's God entitle them, a decent respect to the opinions of mankind requires that they should declare the causes which impel them to the separation.

We hold these truths to be self-evident, that all men are created equal, that they are endowed by their Creator with certain unalienable Rights, that among these are Life, Liberty and the pursuit of Happiness.–That to secure these rights, Governments are instituted among Men, deriving their just powers from the consent of the governed, –That whenever any Form of Government becomes destructive of these ends, it is the Right of the People to alter or to abolish it, and to institute new Government, laying its foundation on such principles and organizing its powers in such form, as to them shall seem most likely to effect their Safety and Happiness. Prudence, indeed, will dictate that Governments long established should not be changed for light and transient causes; and accordingly all experience hath shewn, that mankind are more disposed to suffer, while evils are sufferable, than to right themselves by abolishing the forms to which they are accustomed. But when a long train of abuses and usurpations, pursuing invariably the same Object evinces a design to reduce them under absolute Despotism, it is their right, it is their duty, to throw off such Government, and to provide new Guards for their future security.–Such has been the patient sufferance of these Colonies; and such is now the necessity which constrains them to alter their former Systems of Government. The history of the present King of Great Britain is a history of repeated injuries and usurpations, all having in direct object the establishment of an absolute Tyranny over these States. To prove this, let Facts be submitted to a candid world.

He has refused his Assent to Laws, the most wholesome and necessary for the public good.

He has forbidden his Governors to pass Laws of immediate and pressing importance, unless suspended in their operation till his Assent should be obtained; and when so suspended, he has utterly neglected to attend to them.

He has refused to pass other Laws for the accommodation of large districts of people, unless those people would relinquish the right of Representation in the Legislature, a right inestimable to them and formidable to tyrants only.

He has called together legislative bodies at places unusual, uncomfortable, and distant from the depository of their public Records, for the sole purpose of fatiguing them into compliance with his measures.

He has dissolved Representative Houses repeatedly, for opposing with manly firmness his invasions on the rights of the people.

He has refused for a long time, after such dissolutions, to cause others to be elected; whereby the Legislative powers, incapable of Annihilation, have returned to the People at large for their exercise; the State remaining in the mean time exposed to all the dangers of invasion from without, and convulsions within.

He has endeavoured to prevent the population of these States; for that purpose obstructing the Laws for Naturalization of Foreigners; refusing to pass others to encourage their migrations hither, and raising the conditions of new Appropriations of Lands.

He has obstructed the Administration of Justice, by refusing his Assent to Laws for establishing Judiciary powers.

He has made Judges dependent on his Will alone, for the tenure of their offices, and the amount and payment of their salaries.

He has erected a multitude of New Offices, and sent hither swarms of Officers to harrass our people, and eat out their substance.

He has kept among us, in times of peace, Standing Armies without the Consent of our legislatures.

He has affected to render the Military independent of and superior to the Civil power.

He has combined with others to subject us to a jurisdiction foreign to our constitution, and unacknowledged by our laws; giving his Assent to their Acts of pretended Legislation:

For Quartering large bodies of armed troops among us:

For protecting them, by a mock Trial, from punishment for any Murders which they should commit on the Inhabitants of these States:

For cutting off our Trade with all parts of the world:

For imposing Taxes on us without our Consent:

For depriving us in many cases, of the benefits of Trial by Jury:

For transporting us beyond Seas to be tried for pretended offences

For abolishing the free System of English Laws in a neighbouring Province, establishing therein an Arbitrary government, and enlarging its Boundaries so as to render it at once an example and fit instrument for introducing the same absolute rule into these Colonies:

For taking away our Charters, abolishing our most valuable Laws, and altering fundamentally the Forms of our Governments:

For suspending our own Legislatures, and declaring themselves invested with power to legislate for us in all cases whatsoever.

He has abdicated Government here, by declaring us out of his Protection and waging War against us.

He has plundered our seas, ravaged our Coasts, burnt our towns, and destroyed the lives of our people.

He is at this time transporting large Armies of foreign Mercenaries to compleat the works of death, desolation and tyranny, already begun with circumstances of Cruelty & perfidy scarcely paralleled in the most barbarous ages, and totally unworthy the Head of a civilized nation.

He has constrained our fellow Citizens taken Captive on the high Seas to bear Arms against their Country, to become the executioners of their friends and Brethren, or to fall themselves by their Hands.

He has excited domestic insurrections amongst us, and has endeavoured to bring on the inhabitants of our frontiers, the merciless Indian Savages, whose known rule of warfare, is an undistinguished destruction of all ages, sexes and conditions.

In every stage of these Oppressions We have Petitioned for Redress in the most humble terms: Our repeated Petitions have been answered only by repeated injury. A Prince whose character is thus marked by every act which may define a Tyrant, is unfit to be the ruler of a free people.

Nor have We been wanting in attentions to our Brittish brethren. We have warned them from time to time of attempts by their legislature to extend an unwarrantable jurisdiction over us. We have reminded them of the circumstances of our emigration and settlement here. We have appealed to their native justice and magnanimity, and we have conjured them by the ties of our common kindred to disavow these usurpations, which, would inevitably interrupt our connections and correspondence. They too have been deaf to the voice of justice and of consanguinity. We must, therefore, acquiesce in the necessity, which denounces our Separation, and hold them, as we hold the rest of mankind, Enemies in War, in Peace Friends.

We, therefore, the Representatives of the united States of America, in General Congress, Assembled, appealing to the Supreme Judge of the world for the rectitude of our intentions, do, in the Name, and by Authority of the good People of these Colonies, solemnly publish and declare, That these United Colonies are, and of Right ought to be Free and Independent States; that they are Absolved from all Allegiance to the British Crown, and that all political connection between them and the State of Great Britain, is and ought to be totally dissolved; and that as Free and Independent States, they have full Power to levy War, conclude Peace, contract Alliances, establish Commerce, and to do all other Acts and Things which Independent States may of right do. And for the support of this Declaration, with a firm reliance on the protection of divine Providence, we mutually pledge to each other our Lives, our Fortunes and our sacred Honor.

July 4, 1776

Signers of the Declaration of Independence

Georgia

Button Gwinnett, Lyman Hall and George Walton

North Carolina

William Hooper, Joseph Hewes and John Penn

South Carolina

Edward Rutledge, Thomas Heyward, Jr., Thomas Lynch, Jr. and Arthur Middleton

Massachusetts

Samuel Adams, John Adams, Robert Treat Paine and Elbridge Gerry and John Hancock

Maryland

Samuel Chase, William Paca, Thomas Stone and

Charles Carroll of Carrollton

Virginia

George Wythe, Richard Henry Lee, Thomas Jefferson, Benjamin Harrison Thomas Nelson Jr., Francis Lightfoot Lee and

Carter Braxton

Pennsylvania

Robert Morris, Benjamin Rush, Benjamin Franklin, John Morton, George Clymer, James Smith, George Taylor, James Wilson and George Ross

Delaware

Caesar Rodney, George Read and Thomas McKean

New York

William Floyd, Philip Livingston, Francis Lewis and Lewis Morris

New Jersey

Richard Stockton, John Witherspoon, Francis Hopkinson, John Hart and Abraham Clark

New Hampshire

Josiah Bartlett, William Whipple and Matthew Thornton

Rhode Island

Stephen Hopkins and William Ellery

Connecticut

Roger Sherman, Samuel Huntington, William Williams and Oliver Wolcott

The Declaration of Independence was signed in the Pennsylvania State House that would be renamed Independence Hall. The name, Independence Hall, powerfully captures the result of this historic event that could have ended in disaster. This document is the birth certificate of America. This thirty-five word statement, "We hold these truths to be self-evident, that all men are created equal, that they are endowed by their Creator with certain unalienable Rights, that among these are Life, Liberty and the pursuit of Happiness," sums up what makes America exceptional.

After independence was declared, the problems for this new country only worsened. George Washington constantly struggled with the Second Continental Congress for money, food, and arms. Many in Congress were trying to micromanage the war by controlling Washington's battle plans and his soldiers. Because this document also served as a declaration of war against Great Britain, America was at war with a superior enemy. The British had the best-trained and equipped army in the world; and at this point in the war the British were winning. Finally, the signers of the Declaration of Independence were now committing treason. They were laying their lives and fortunes on the line. America's defeat would mean their certain death.

The French

Many French citizens desired freedom from King Louis XVI after America's successful fight with England. The French's fight for freedom, however, had different challenges than the ones faced by America. The French people had lived under the rule of kings for centuries. Being ruled was part of their national identity. The leaders of the French Revolution were very different from the founders in America. The Americans were experienced soldiers and politicians. They were wealthy businessmen and many were highly educated. Some of the revolutionary leaders in France were educated but had little experience in politics or warfare. Many of the leaders were from the third estate, and they had few resources and limited experience in leading. Even their notions of liberty were vastly different. Susan Dunn states in *Sister Revolutions*, "Indeed, he [Tocqueville] remarked that political philosophy had led in America to Liberty, while in France it merely invented new forms of servitude."[1] Dunn continues, "Saint-Just proclaimed, 'What constitutes a republic is the total destruction of everything that stands in opposition to it.'"[2]

The French Declared Their Freedom

July 14, 1789—Storming of the Bastille

The Bastille was the infamous Royal prison in Paris. The storming of the Bastille not only symbolized a direct attack against King Louis XVI, but the Bastille also stored weapons and gunpowder that the people wanted to use in their fight against the king and his supporters.

August 26, 1789—The Declaration of Rights of Man and Citizen Approved

This document had several implications. First, all privileges and feudal rights were abolished. Second, the nation of France became sovereign and all men equal under the law. Last, the unity of the people was the most important factor in this new order. Unity meant that the nation of France existed as "one" and was indivisible. Below is a copy of the Declaration of the Rights of Man and Citizen. Please read it and notice the differences between this document and our Declaration of Independence.

Declaration of the Rights of Man and Citizen- 1789

The representatives of the French people, organized as a National Assembly, believing that the ignorance, neglect, or contempt of the rights of man are the sole cause of public calamities and of the corruption of governments, have determined to set forth in a solemn declaration the natural, unalienable, and sacred rights of man, in order that this declaration, being constantly before all the members of the Social body, shall remind them continually of their rights and duties; in order that the acts of the legislative power, as well as those of the executive power, may be compared at any moment with the objects and purposes of all political institutions and may thus be more respected, and, lastly, in order that the grievances of the citizens, based hereafter upon simple and incontestable principles, shall tend to the maintenance of the constitution and redound to the happiness of all. Therefore the National Assembly recognizes and proclaims, in the presence and under the auspices of the Supreme Being, the following rights of man and of the citizen:

Articles:

1. Men are born and remain free and equal in rights. Social distinctions may be founded only upon the general good.

2. The aim of all political association is the preservation of the natural and imprescriptible rights of man. These rights are liberty, property, security, and resistance to oppression.

3. The principle of all sovereignty resides essentially in the nation. No

body nor individual may exercise any authority which does not proceed directly from the nation.

4. Liberty consists in the freedom to do everything which injures no one else; hence the exercise of the natural rights of each man has no limits except those which assure to the other members of the society the enjoyment of the same rights. These limits can only be determined by law.

5. Law can only prohibit such actions as are hurtful to society. Nothing may be prevented which is not forbidden by law, and no one may be forced to do anything not provided for by law.

6. Law is the expression of the general will. Every citizen has a right to participate personally, or through his representative, in its foundation. It must be the same for all, whether it protects or punishes. All citizens, being equal in the eyes of the law, are equally eligible to all dignities and to all public positions and occupations, according to their abilities, and without distinction except that of their virtues and talents.

7. No person shall be accused, arrested, or imprisoned except in the cases and according to the forms prescribed by law. Any one soliciting, transmitting, executing, or causing to be executed, any arbitrary order, shall be punished. But any citizen summoned or arrested in virtue of the law shall submit without delay, as resistance constitutes an offense.

8. The law shall provide for such punishments only as are strictly and obviously necessary, and no one shall suffer punishment except it be legally inflicted in virtue of a law passed and promulgated before the

commission of the offense.

9. As all persons are held innocent until they shall have been declared guilty, if arrest shall be deemed indispensable, all harshness not essential to the securing of the prisoner's person shall be severely repressed by law.

10. No one shall be disquieted on account of his opinions, including his religious views, provided their manifestation does not disturb the public order established by law.

11. The free communication of ideas and opinions is one of the most precious of the rights of man. Every citizen may, accordingly, speak, write, and print with freedom, but shall be responsible for such abuses of this freedom as shall be defined by law.

12. The security of the rights of man and of the citizen requires public military forces. These forces are, therefore, established for the good of all and not for the personal advantage of those to whom they shall be intrusted.

13. A common contribution is essential for the maintenance of the public forces and for the cost of administration. This should be equitably distributed among all the citizens in proportion to their means.

14. All the citizens have a right to decide, either personally or by their representatives, as to the necessity of the public contribution; to grant this freely; to know to what uses it is put; and to fix the proportion, the mode of assessment and of collection and the duration of the taxes.

15. Society has the right to require of every public agent an account of his administration.

16. A society in which the observance of the law is not assured, nor the separation of powers defined, has no constitution at all.

17. Since property is an inviolable and sacred right, no one shall be deprived thereof except where public necessity, legally determined, shall clearly demand it, and then only on condition that the owner shall have been previously and equitably indemnified.

Approved by the National Assembly of France, August 26, 1789

October 5, 1789—Women's March on Versailles

Some seven thousand women in Paris—angry over the cost and scarcity of bread—joined together in a spontaneous march on Versailles. Not only did the women protest concerning the lack of bread and its price, they also called upon the monarch to move his operation from Versailles to Paris in order to be closer to his people. King Louis XVI bowed to the women's demands and on the next day, under the protection of Lafayette and his National Guard, moved the royal family to Paris.

August 10, 1792—The French Monarchy Ended

The Palace of Tuileries, the residence of the royal family, was attacked by thousands of angry French citizens, and the king and his family were defended by his guards from the Swiss Guard and the *Gaide du Corps*. Thousands died in this battle. The royal family was captured and the monarchy suspended.

January 21, 1793—King Louis XVI Executed

King Louis XVI was executed by means of the guillotine, the most popular form of capital punishment during the French Revolution. Susan Dunn remarks, "Only after the abolition of the monarchy, in the fall of 1792, would the people reign alone. The beheading of Louis XVI was the crowning of the people as the new indivisible, infallible sovereign."[3]

March 9-10, 1793—The Revolutionary Tribunal

The Revolutionary Tribunal was a court established to ferret out domestic enemies and all other threats to national unity. The tribunal was composed of a jury, a prosecutor, and two substitutes who were nominated by the Convention. The power of this group was used against enemies of the revolution and personal enemies of the revolutionary leadership. This tribunal killed between 17,000 and 50,000 people.

April 6, 1793

The Committee on Public Safety takes control of the French government.

June 24, 1793

The new constitution of France was ratified by the National Convention.

September 17, 1793–July 28, 1794—Reign of Terror

The beginning of the French Revolution was violent. The Reign of Terror in France led to the execution of tens of thousands of people. At the heart of the Reign of Terror was the Committee of Public Safety headed by Maximilien Robespierre. This group was charged with protecting the revolution at all costs. The Reign of Terror ended with Robespierre's death.

The Story Continues

It is one thing to declare your freedom as a group of like-minded coloni-alists who desired to "form a more perfect union" or a group of revolution-aries desiring the simple necessities of life, but winning and maintaining that freedom is a far greater challenge. Freedom that requires war is not free. In a war that would last over eight years and a revolution and Reign of Terror that would cost thousands of lives, the price paid is incalculable.

In the next chapter we pause from our study of France and America. We will define what true freedom is and see that true freedom is free indeed.

CHAPTER 3
Freedom Defined

Humanity's sin is the root cause of all the problems and brutality faced by mankind for all time. Sin has placed humanity in spiritual bondage. You cannot always see the shackles and chains that bind us, but they are real. This deadly bondage has catastrophic and eternal consequences. Without the grace of God through the life, death, and resurrection of Jesus Christ, there is no hope of breaking free from this bondage.

At this point in our story, it is important to pause and take a closer look at the two primary themes found in the *Liberty Keys*: bondage or tyranny and freedom or liberty. As we review these themes, we will look at them from two different vantage points, one political and the other spiritual.

Two Types of Bondage

Political Bondage

For our purposes, political bondage is defined as the bondage that is imposed upon one person by another or by a government upon its citizens. History shows that this type of bondage can divide or destroy individuals and nations. The *Liberty Keys* describes two examples of political bondage. First, under the monarchy of King George III, the American colonies were held in a type of long-distance bondage primarily through laws, taxes, and the threat of military action. Second, King Louis XVI controlled the citizens of France under the bondage of his inept leadership. His mismanagement created general unrest because of shortages of money and food. While the king and the first estate (the nobility) were living in luxury, the third estate (the people of France) were poor and hungry. In time, these circumstances led to the breakdown of French society and created an atmosphere ripe for revolution.

The most horrifying example of political bondage is slavery. Throughout history slavery has been all too common, disgraceful, and deadly. Humans, created in the image of God are owned by other humans and forced to work under the threat of harm or death while at the same time enriching their owners.

A more recent example of political bondage is communism. In the Soviet Union the government controlled every aspect of Soviet society for the "common good." The leaders created a godless society where its people lived under the threat of imprisonment or death for any behavior that posed a threat to the state. The party leaders lived in comfort and excess while the citizens lived in meager government housing, earned controlled wages, and had limited access to resources. The goal of the Communist Revolution was to defeat freedom and control the world.

Even in a post-Soviet world, political bondage remains. It may not be as blatant and reprehensible as slavery or as destructive as communism, but it can be extremely harmful to societies as a whole and to the individuals directly involved. An example of this type of bondage is socialism. Citizens of socialist countries have a taste of freedom but have limited choices in education and employment. In socialist countries the government controls major segments of society, including health care and industry. These citizens may think that they are free, but unlike the citizens of the United

States, their freedom is restricted to set, predetermined boundaries established by the government.

In most cases today political bondage is imposed by the heavy hands of government. Political leaders, in their pursuit of tyrannical control over their citizens, commit countless injustices that have at their root the sins of pride, murder, greed, and lust. These sins and others destroy individuals, families, and nations. War and tyranny are simply the visible reality of the destructive power of sin committed by both well-intentioned and blatantly evil political leaders.

Spiritual Bondage

The second type of bondage is spiritual. This type of bondage is much more difficult to see and understand. Humanity cannot agree upon its cause or even its existence. This is a controversial issue because it is directly linked to an individual's personal belief concerning at least three points: the holy Bible as absolute truth, every person as a sinner, and finally eternity. Because the Liberty Keys is written from a Christian's perspective, there is one key verse that sums up the Bible's view concerning the issue of spiritual bondage: "For the wages of sin is death . . ." (Rom 6:23a). In other words, non-Christ followers' payment or punishment for unforgiven sin is an eternity in hell, a place of complete separation from God. Matthew 8:12 says this about hell: "But the sons of the kingdom will be cast out into the outer darkness; in that place there will be weeping and gnashing of teeth."

Genesis relates how spiritual bondage began. The man (Adam) received instructions from God allowing him to eat from every tree in the garden except one. "Then the Lord God took the man and put him into the Garden of Eden to cultivate it and keep it. The Lord God commanded the man, saying, 'From any tree of the garden you may eat freely; but from the tree of the knowledge of good and evil you shall not eat, for in the day that you eat from it you will surely die'" (Gen 2:15–17). Satan slithered into the story in Genesis 3. Satan caused the woman (Eve) to question God's words to the man. The woman saw that the food from the tree was good, and she ate some and also gave some to her husband.

Instantly, everything changed. The world and everything in it would be radically different until the end of time. No longer was mankind at peace with God. Sin severed the bonds that were established between God and mankind at creation. The eternal truths of Romans 3:23, "for all have sinned and fall short of the glory of God," and Romans 6:23a, "For the wages of sin is death . . .," can trace their sobering power back to this story in Genesis. Would God allow humanity to be without any hope for all eternity? No! God has always had a plan to deal with our sin and it is called grace. There will be more about grace later.

Two Types of Freedom

Political Freedom

The first type of freedom is political freedom. Generally defined, political freedom is the freedom people have within the culture or country in which they live. The only limits that are placed upon the individual are set by family, society, and the government.

The founder's design for the United States of America was first revealed to the world in the opening words of the Declaration of

Independence: "We hold these truths to be self-evident, that all men are created equal, that they are endowed by their Creator with certain unalienable rights that among these are life, liberty and the pursuit of happiness." America is unique because it was founded on the simple principle that its citizens are free. As Americans, we are free to elect our political leaders. We are free to determine our futures. We are free to worship as we choose. We are free to live our lives with little interference from the government. With the exception of America, all other societies, past and present, were established by rulers or kings who subjected their citizens to various degrees of tyranny. Under the banners of kingdoms, socialism, Nazism, communism, and other systems of government, citizens were and remain under various degrees of state control. In these places the laws of the government do not restrict the government's rights over its citizens but rather limit the people's liberty under the law. In America, the founders wrote the Constitution to limit the power of the government to control the liberties of the people.

The best example of political freedom is the freedom we have in America. As Americans we can, for the most part, choose our own futures, i.e., the American Dream. We can choose where we want to live. Beyond a certain age, we can choose our level of education. We can pick our careers. There are only two primary limits to our freedom. First, are we willing to work hard enough to acquire the American Dream? Second, are we willing to live within the rule of law, the United States Constitution?

We must remember that America's freedom isn't free. Men and women for generations have paid a heavy price for our freedom. Forgotten heroes fighting on countless battlefields have faithfully maintained the freedom we enjoy. To intentionally or by neglect give up our freedom is an insult to the memory of our founding fathers and our veterans.

Spiritual Freedom

The second type of freedom, in my view the most important freedom for all humanity and for all time, is spiritual freedom. This freedom is only found in a personal relationship with Jesus Christ. The liberty that Christ followers have in Jesus Christ is only received as a gift from God. That gift is called grace. The Bible speaks about grace in Romans 6:23b, ". . . but the free gift of God is eternal life in Christ Jesus our Lord." No amount of work, money, fame, or celebrity can allow someone to receive grace. The biblical reality is that people who do not have this free gift are so blinded by their own sin and false religious teaching that they do not even know that they need grace. God is the one who reveals to people, through the Holy Spirit, their need for grace. God is the one who provides this grace through his resurrection of Jesus Christ from the dead. God is also the one who gives the gift of grace to people because of the faith they demonstrate by confession of sin. The end result is spiritual freedom.

Spiritual freedom gives Christ followers two places to serve God: on earth and in heaven. First, Christ followers can serve God for every moment remaining on the earth. Christ followers should count it a wonderful privilege to serve God through obedience to his word, the Bible. For example, the Bible tells Christ followers in Matthew 28:19 to "make disciples of all the nations." This is a wonderful and sometimes overwhelming task that we must work to complete. Second, after our physical death we have the absolute guarantee of spending eternity in heaven serving God. Serving God in whatever capacity he commands will be an unspeakable joy. We only have that guarantee because of the relationship that was established while on earth with God through Jesus Christ.

How to Receive Spiritual Freedom

If we cannot do anything to reestablish our relationship with God, how can anyone go to heaven? Everything would appear to be hopeless. The single sin of one person ruined everything for everybody. Surely God would not punish everyone for a little bite of fruit? Because of this sin, what would happen to the garden? Because of this sin, what would happen to the rest of creation?

The freedom Christ followers have in Jesus Christ is not anything deserved or earned; it is a gift. All adherents of every world religion, with the exception of Christianity, must "work" to earn their salvation or "work" to keep it. What does that mean? Working for your salvation involves following a religion's list of prescribed rules or steps to receive or keep that religion's promise of some form of eternal life.

To reestablish your relationship with God, there are two exclusive participants: God and the sinner. God's part in this process is by far the primary one. Our part, the sinner's part, seems very small. The Bible makes it very clear that both parts are required for the reestablishment of the sinner's relationship with God to last for all eternity.

God's Part

Perhaps no other verse in the entire Bible shows God's role in the process of salvation more clearly than John 3:16. This beloved verse states, "For God so loved the world, that He gave His only begotten Son, that whoever believes in Him shall not perish, but have eternal life." The freedom that we have in Christ is made possible because of the love that God the Father has for us. The love God has for people required several action steps on His part. Because I could almost count ever word in the Bible as an action step, please note that this list of steps is not the detailed list of every step or act, but the absolute necessary ones God took to reestablish His relationship with sinners.

Step One

God's first step was to send Jesus to earth. The story of Jesus coming to earth was predicted in Scripture and became a reality for a young couple in Bethlehem named Joseph and Mary. Now the story of Jesus's birth is celebrated by countless millions all around the world.

Step Two

After his baptism Jesus began his three-and-a-half-year ministry of "seeking and saving the lost." He continued His perfect obedience to the plans and actions that God the Father had given him to complete. Jesus's perfect obedience to God the Father affirmed that Jesus was the "perfect lamb of God." Jesus would now be able to become the only one who could reestablish God's relationship with sinners.

Step Three

Jesus had accomplished everything his father told Him to do. According to God's plan, it was now time for the sinless Son of God to die for sinful humanity. Jesus's death was the price required by God for the payment of all the sins of humanity. The manner of his death—the cross—was the most brutal means of death ever devised by mankind. Jesus died sur-rounded by a criminal on each side. He was buried in a borrowed tomb. Every one of Jesus's followers abandoned him, along with his Father.

Step Four

God's next step required the most amazing act of all. God did not leave Jesus, his beloved Son, in the grave. God raised Jesus from the dead. Romans 10:9 says, " if you confess with your mouth Jesus as Lord, and believe in your heart that God raised Him for the dead, you will be saved." On the third day, God resurrected Jesus from the dead. This one action is the most important event in human history. Without the resurrection of Jesus Christ, there is no forgiveness. There is no hope for salvation.

Our Part

In order to have freedom in Jesus Christ, a person must accept Jesus Christ as his or her Lord and Savior by faith. Below is a simple list of Scripture passages that will help you understand how to become a Christ Follower.

1. You are a sinner (Rom 3:23)

    "for all have sinned and fall short of the glory of God."

2. You will pay the price for your sin (Rom 6:23a)

    "For the wages of sin is death,"

3. Jesus Christ paid the price for your sin (Rom 5:8)

    "But God demonstrates His own love toward us, in that while we were yet sinners, Christ died for us."

4. You have God's promise of forgiveness (Rom 10:13)

"For 'WHOEVER WILL CALL ON THE NAME
OF THE LORD WILL BE SAVED,'"

5. You must confess and believe to be forgiven (Rom 10: 9–10)

*"if you confess with your mouth Jesus as Lord, and believe in
your heart that God raised Him from the dead, you will be saved;
for with the heart a person believes, resulting in righteousness,
and with the mouth he confesses, resulting in salvation."*

6. You must now pray, asking God for forgiveness of sin by faith

Dear Father,
I know that I am a sinner. I know that the
punishment for my sin is an eternity in
hell. I need forgiveness of my sin today. I believe
that Jesus died on the cross even
though He did not sin. I believe that He died
in my place. I also believe that You
raised Him from the dead after three days in
the grave. Father, please forgive me
of all my sins. I want to make Jesus the Lord
of my life. I want to live for You for
the rest of my life. I now know that when I
die that I will spend eternity in
heaven with You. Thank you for my forgiveness and I ask for it
in the name of Jesus Christ. Amen.

If you prayed that prayer, you are now free in Jesus Christ. Now you can tell others that you have received forgiveness of sin in the name of Jesus Christ. Now you can tell them how they can receive freedom in Jesus Christ. The remainder of this study should have new meaning and value for you. There can be no doubt that Jesus Christ can be called the Great Liberator. With his death and glorious resurrection, Jesus liberated all who have called upon his name for forgiveness of sin. The value of this action is priceless.

The Story Continues

For decades our country has been moving away from our founding principles that have made us a great nation. Our nation has been on a journey leading to our demise. Now is the time to stop this journey and reverse course. Now is time for you to help return the United States of America to our founding principles found in the Declaration of Independence and the United States Constitution.

CHAPTER 4
Freedom's Demise

France

The sweet melody of liberty is not so sweet everywhere it is heard. Like a prophet of the Old Testament, Reverend Samuel Cooper warned the Frenchmen who returned home after partnering with the colonialists to secure independence and freedom for America about how their zeal for liberty would find few allies back home in France. James Gains in his book, *For Liberty and Glory*, shares Cooper's warning:

> Two weeks before sailing back to France, he was in Boston with a group of twenty other returning French officers when they visited with the Reverend Samuel Cooper, the eloquent, Francophile pastor of Boston's Brattle Square Church. When the officers spoke eagerly about the triumph of liberty, Cooper cut them short. "Take care, young men," he said. "You carry home with you the seeds of liberty, but if you attempt to plant them in a country that has been corrupt for so long, you will face obstacles far more formidable that we did. We spilled a great deal of blood to win our liberty, but to establish it in the old world, you will shed it in torrents."[1]

The results of the French Revolution should give all Americans a wakeup call concerning the priceless nature of freedom. The French Revolution was a tragic mess. The lessons learned should stop America's journey back into tyranny dead in its tracks. If the goal of the French Revolution was to secure freedom for future generations of French citizens, then it was a complete failure. Susan Dunn states, "After centuries of the wrenching inequality of a rigid, elitist caste system, revolutionaries in France hungered first and foremost for equality. While the Americans' driving passion was for freedom, in France people longed for a nation of equal citizens."[2] Dunn continues, "Indeed, Rousseau's utopian, ethical, democratic polity includes no channels for the expression of dissent or opposition. Having defined the General Will as infallible and sovereign."[3] The lofty goals of the revolutionary leaders were based on a false premise, and that is why the revolution failed. The results of this revolution were death, destruction, and a new tyrannical leader of the French people, Napoleon Bonaparte.

The history of France between the execution of King Louis XVI on January 21, 1793, and Napoleon Bonaparte declaring himself Emperor of France on May 18, 1804, is just over ten years. The events packed into those years, including eight different constitutions, are too numerous to review here. As we conclude our look at France's failed attempt for liberty, below are some key events regarding France's fall back into tyranny.

August 22, 1795

The French Constitution is ratified by the National Convention. It calls for a five-man directory and an upper and lower house of the parliament.

September 23, 1795

The new Constitution of the Year II goes into effect in France.

November 9, 1799

Napoleon Bonaparte overthrows the directory.

December 12, 1799

The Constitution of the Year VIII proclaimed Napoleon Bonaparte the First Consul of France.

May 18, 1804

Napoleon declares himself emperor of France.

America

Music is powerful. It can touch the hearts of people and nations like nothing else. When I think about the music that captures the heart, hope, pride, and blessings of America, I think of two songs. The first song is none other than our national anthem, "The Star-Spangled Banner," by Francis Scott Key. The music and the words of the first verse can be heard in every corner of America. It is heard at most public gatherings and has been memorized by young and old for generations. I don't know if you need the words, but I have included them below. Don't forget to stand while you read or sing these cherished words.

O say can you see, by the dawn's early light,
What so proudly we hailed at the twilight's last gleaming?
Whose broad stripes and bright stars through the perilous fight,
O'er the ramparts we watched were so gallantly streaming?
And the rocket's red glare, the bomb bursting in air,

Gave proof through the night that our flag was still there.

O say does that star-spangled banner yet wave

O'er the land of the free, and the home of the brave?

The second song that captures America's dependence upon God for his blessings and gives everyone a feeling of hope is none other than "God Bless America" by Irving Berlin. This magnificent song describes a journey from one coast to the other and America's need for and an appreciation of God's blessings. This song, written 100 years ago, captures the spirit of humility and dependence we must have in order to receive God's blessings. If you know the tune, sing it. If you don't know the tune, enjoy the simple lyrics.

God bless America, Land that I love,

Stand beside her and guide her

Through the night with a light from above;

From the mountains, to the prairies,

To the oceans white with foam,

God bless America, My home, sweet home.

God bless America, My home, sweet home.

The nostalgia and hope created by the words of these two wonderful and powerful songs is sadly being drowned out by the louder sound of negative change and decline that America is experiencing. Since the 2016 elections, however, there are signs of positive change across the land. For many Americans, there is optimism and a genuine hope for the restoration of America. For others, America must not erase changes made by the progressive agenda of the previous administration. For the hopeful, there is still a great amount of work to be done for the country to be healed.

For those who were defeated and angry about the outcome of the 2016 elections, there is a radical or even revolutionary desire not to accept the outcome of the election and fight against any and all decisions made by the new administration. They are unwilling to remain peaceful and live under the rule of law. They refuse to fight only through the ballot box or the court room. Our division continues to grow. The root cause of this divide is masked by challenging and painful issues such as racism and inequality. All evidence points to political ideology as the primary cause for the division in America. We are in the middle of an Uncivil Civil War in America. Our freedom does not shield us from disunity and conflicts. We need to hear the words of O.S. Guinness from his book A *Free People's Suicide*: "For at the heart of freedom lies a grand paradox: *the greatest enemy of freedom is freedom*."[4] Our Uncivil Civil War has two fronts. The first battle front is Citizens vs. Citizens. The second battle front is Citizens vs. Government.

Citizens vs. Citizens

On September 9, 1776, the Continental Congress formally named our nation the United States of America. The colonies had formerly been referred to as the United Colonies. Thomas Jefferson is credited with naming our nation the United States of America, as its first formal use is found in the Declaration of Independence. Our name teaches us how we are to coexist with our fellow Americans. United! We are the *United* States of America. We must live up to our name. Our behavior is anything but united. United does not mean conformity under tyranny, but it does mean being unified under the rule of law.

On June 14, 1777, the Continental Congress passed the first Flag Act. It states, "Resolved, That the flag of the United States be made of thirteen stripes, alternate red and white; that the union by thirteen stars, white in a blue field, representing a new Constellation." The Flag Act of April 4, 1818, provided for thirteen stripes and one star for each state, to be added to the flag on the fourth of July following the admission of each new state. The flag represents our nation. The pledge of allegiance expresses, in the best possible way, how the flag represents our nation and what our nation is to be. Please stand and make your pledge.

Pledge of Allegiance

I pledge allegiance to the flag of the
United States of America,
and to the republic for which it stands,
one nation under God, indivisible,
with liberty and justice for all.

Our pledge states that we are "one nation under God" and "indivisible." Every time we recite the pledge of allegiance to the flag of the United States, we are claiming that we are one nation under God and that we are indivisible. To see America with our own eyes and hear the news reports, America is anything but one and indivisible.

Our citizens are divided. This division is taught and perpetuated by a liberal and anti-traditional American values bias in our media and by much of our government and education system. For example, our news media will take elements of a story that involves a police officer and a youth who are from different races and make the story about race rather than about the enforcement of the law. The story will become fake news designed to create racial tension in a particular community or the nation. Activist teachers share their revisionist history, anti-religion, or political bias to their students, regardless of grade level or parental permission. These lessons become indoctrination sessions that in many ways harm the students' understanding of historical facts, demean their ability to discern the truth, and continue the division of Americans. Other issues are just as harmful to our need to be a unified country. Some of the issues include gang violence, inner-city poverty and crime, illegal immigration, and attacks aimed at our law enforcement officers. Activists live by this philosophy, "If I don't get my way, I will protest." We must be united and live in peace with one another under the rule of law before it is too late.

Citizens vs. Government

In many sectors of society, our country is barely surviving. Economic and cultural conditions are bad in many parts of the nation. Americans citizens are bombarded by misleading messages from the government and their media partners about the state of our country. These messages conflict with our own observation and experience. Don't misunderstand me; America is by far the greatest nation in the world. Our history of freedom and defending freedom is unmatched. Our system of government, as established in the United States Constitution, helps us maintain our freedom and affords Americans the best standard of living in the world; but, after years of mismanagement by selfish and arrogant politicians, our country has fallen on hard times. Our entrenched leaders say, "Our economy is strong. Jobs are plentiful. You have more than enough money to have a standard of living higher than most people in the world. It is better for the environment if you to learn to live with less. This is the new normal."

The struggle in America is no longer party against party. The struggle is now between those who desire America to remain as founded and designed and those who want to change America into something that satisfies their own personal desires of wealth and security. Our system is corrupted. A deadly partnership has formed around the sins of greed and power. The partnership is made up of politicians who are willing to sell their integrity, their offices, and the future of America to the highest bidder. The other side of this partnership is special interest groups, lobbyists, and voters looking for special treatment or a portion of the money controlled by the politicians. The special interest groups and lobbyists tell the politicians, "Give us what we want or we will stop funding your re-election campaigns or cancel our promise to you of a high paying job when you leave office." The voters tell the politicians, "You give us what we want and we will keep you in office." This partnership has created a group of people who are choosing between working and receiving government benefits. This group is asking themselves, "Should I work today? All of my bills are paid. Why should I work when someone else is paying me to stay home?" Both sides want to keep each other happy regardless of the cost or the damage to the very foundation of America.

A powerful and tyrannical government has several deadly weapons in their arsenal for the fight against its own citizens. They use taxes and regulations to control monetary growth and industry and manipulated statistics and bad science to control the truth. They can try to lie to us, but we know the truth. We are the ones buying food that has become much more expensive. We are the ones driving our cars that are hard to keep on the road because of their price and operating cost. We are the ones trying to buy or sell a home. We are the ones dealing with our grown children trapped at home with large student loans that put them behind before they even get started in life. Our families, friends, and neighbors have given up looking for jobs or have retired early with a fraction of their former income. There may be jobs available, but many are part-time because of turmoil created by the Affordable Care Act. People are working in jobs, not careers, or working more than one job to make ends meet.

Does it matter to these politicians that we have a national debt that is out of control? Does it matter to them that Social Security is just a few years from collapse? Does it matter to them that the vast majority of Americans are living from paycheck to paycheck? Does it matter to them that most Americans have an overwhelming amount of personal debt?

Sadly, too many Americans do not care that our government officials and a small number of their friends and accomplices are living well and getting rich. This small group of elites will always have their needs and wants satisfied. Many politicians enter office in debt and magically become wealthy on a fixed government salary. They have created a system within the larger system of the rule of law that benefits them and their friends. We are reliving our pre-Revolutionary War history. A few powerful governmental leaders are imposing a new brand of tyranny upon Americans.

It would appear that the majority of Americans have fallen under a spell. This spell has blinded their ability to see what is happening to our country. This spell has turned many Americans, too many Americans, into selfish citizens who have no desire to be responsible and productive. Susan Dunn comments about the problem with this mindset in *Sister Revolutions*: "But citizen's preoccupation with their own narrow self-interest, their obsession with acquisition and accumulation, seduce them and lead them astray-away from participation in self-government and in a dynamic political community."[5] True citizenship involves participation in the free market by working for or owning a business and paying taxes.

It also involves participating in the political process and the big picture ideas of service and sacrifice. These are some of the weapons we can use to fight back against a seemingly out of control government.

We need to be reminded of our past or we are doomed to repeat it. O. S. Guinness also reminds us in his book, A *Free People's Suicide*, "Liberty is therefore a marathon and not a sprint, and the task of freedom requires vigilance and perseverance if freedom is to be sustained."[6] It has not been too many years ago that America was a beacon of freedom. Our parents and grandparents fought against tyranny, and now we are welcoming it back into our lives with open arms. For Americans to be willing to fall back into the tyranny demonstrated by our own government proves that the dangers of tyrannical governments and America's victories over them have been forgotten.

The Endangered States of America

America is a complex nation with many multifaceted problems that must be addressed and resolved for America to survive. The decline America is experiencing threatens our future and it does not involve armies marshaled at our borders. The enemy is within our borders. They are our fellow citizens and guests. Their battle plans are to relentlessly attack our institutions at every level of government, from county courthouses and city halls to the very halls of Congress and the presidency. Violence and intimidation partner with their message as it is proclaimed in the streets. They are patiently and meticulously weaving their anti-American message into the very fabric of our country. Too many Americans are deaf and blind to the real threat to the very existence of our country. O. S. Guinness notes, "Sustainable freedom is urgent for America because freedom is far more difficult to sustain than most Americans realize."[7] Unless Americans begin to listen and see these threats, our country is in real danger.

It is easy to blame others for our lot in life. As citizens of this great country, we must first look at ourselves as part of the reason for our country's decline. We must ask ourselves, "What have I done or not done that has contributed to our decline?" As you continue to ponder your role, let us look at the three primary reasons why America is endangered: our citizens are out of control, our government is out of control, and our media is out of control.

Our Citizens Are Out of Control

The first proof that our citizens are out of control is found in our education system. Much of our education system in America is out of control because parents have left the education of their children to other family members or to complete strangers hired to assume the role of guardian for most of their child's day. With blind trust, disinterest, or laziness, parents have turned over the care and education of their children to the government. The schools are compelled to feed these children up to three meals a day and provide before- and after-school care. Some parents rightly utilize these services because of work and life circumstances, but many parents take advantage of these provided services to have less parental responsibilities. Because of all the time together, the agenda-driven public guardians are able to indoctrinate these children with their values and historical bias. Parents are failing their own children and society as a whole because of their own selfish neglect.

There are groups of parents scattered across the land, whether in public, private, or home school, who do care about the material their children are being taught. Because of their involvement, these parents are criticized and ridiculed by those who desire the progressive indoctrination of America's children. Much of this pushback against these parents comes from union groups who want to keep political power and control over the vast amounts of money spent on education.

The second proof that our citizens are out of control is found in how they desire entertainment. Entertainment has become more than a temporary escape from reality; it is reality. Celebrities are paid large sums of money and worshiped by their fans. Every moment of the day and night, with the aid of personal electronic devices, is filled with entertainment choices. Social media and media on demand have created unlimited choices for consumers. The influence of video games on people of all ages is almost impossible to calculate. Children, youth, and adults are escaping reality and living in fantasy worlds created by books, movies, and theme parks.

The forms of entertainment mentioned above seem harmless compared to the more harmful ones like gambling, drinking alcohol, illegal drug use, and prostitution. Countless Americans are consumed by watching and playing every sport imaginable. This obsession distracts people from dealing with the real issues they must face. Sound financial principles of living within your means and "saving for a rainy day" are lost to people hungry for entertainment. While Americans eat, drink, and make merry, we grow blind to the effects this behavior has on our citizens.

The final proof that our citizens are out of control is found in entitlement programs of the United States government. Granted, entitlement programs can meet the needs of the neediest in our society, but the abuse and fraud of people not in need is incalculable. We live in a "give it to me or I will take it" society. Too many Americans want everything to be free. O. S. Guinness states, "In short, Americans today all seem bent on turning themselves into Uncle Sam's pensioners and are happy to pay any price to do so."[8] Susan Dunn makes this point, "As we 'rush to acquire private wealth or the benefits of the welfare state,' as we focus on consumption and pleasure, we leave the responsibilities of citizenship-concern for the public good, for democratic ideas, for freedom-in the dust."[9]

There are countless people receiving undeserved government hand-outs. The out of control growth and corruption of the food stamp program is one example. More examples of this greed include the fraud of receiving undeserved Social Security benefits, Medicare fraud, and the corruption in filing false tax returns. People are demanding and states are rushing to provide free college tuition. This kind of dependence is harmful to the family and to the nation. The principle of "fair pay for working hard" is disappearing from our country's heritage.

Our Government Is Out of Control

The United States federal government is massive with seemingly unlimited resources. With its size and complexity, it would be impossible to discuss every issue related to it here. However, there are five topics that deserve a brief review that contribute to the government's being in the condition that we find it today.

The first topic concerning our out of control government relates to the judicial branch. This branch, at all levels, was created to interpret the law written by the legislative branch and signed into law by the executive branch. The judiciary is not to write law in the text of their judgments. Mark Levin states in his book *Men in Black*, "The problem, however, remains: judges still routinely usurp power from the other branches of government and act as though they are unconstrained by the Constitution."[10] Judges routinely control the executive branch by stopping executive orders and forcing legal battles. Judges are imposing their political bias upon the other co-equal branches of the government.

The next topic relating to our out of control government concerns the executive branch. The powers of the president of the United States are recorded in the United States Constitution. Article 2–The Executive Branch, Section 1 records the oath of office for the President of the United States. "I do solemnly swear (or affirm) that I will faithfully execute the Office of President of the United States, and will to the best of my Ability, preserve, protect and defend the Constitution of the United States." Any time the president acts outside his enumerated powers, he is breaking the law and his oath of office. It is absolutely necessary for the president to set the tone for the rest of the nation by fulfilling his duties within the rule of law. History proves that presidents, with the aid of their subordinates, have done this all too frequently. History may prove otherwise, but a few examples of this violation include the IRS's targeting of Tea Party organizations and Fast and Furious.

The third topic related to our out-of-control government is the legislative branch. The Congress of the United States has specific constitutional responsibilities. All evidence points to the fact that Congress is not fulfilling that role. Congress has the lowest approval ratings of any branch of government. Congress's primary responsibilities are to write and pass laws to be signed by the president and to control the spending of the government. The government has operated for years without a formal budget. Gridlock and corruption are the two words that best describe Congress. It seems that this group of legislators have no financial accountability or common sense. Our national debt just surpassed twenty trillion dollars. Record tax revenues are pouring into the national treasury, and yet

Congress continues to approve more spending. The American people perceive that the men and women in Congress are serving in politics for their own personal interest and gain. Their goal seems to be doing whatever it takes to keep their job and maintain their power. The persistent mismanagement found in Congress has made America weak and reveals that there are more selfish men and women in Congress than statespeople.

National security is the next issue of concern. Since September 11, 2001, Americans have been willing to give up their freedoms under the banner of national security. The citizens of this great country owe a debt of gratitude to the men and women of our armed services and those who serve in other capacities to keep America safe, but with this word of gratitude comes a word of warning. For example, the creation of the Department of Homeland Security and the enormous power of TSA have led to many of our travel freedoms being reduced and have taken the joy out of air travel. Granted, our security forces are responding to real threats, but there is a fine line between security and a police state. O. S. Guinness states, "Free people are always free to give up freedom in exchange for security. They are not free to pretend they are as free as they were before."[11]

The final topic related to our out of control government is immigration. Contrary to what some citizens and guests of our country believe, America has the most generous immigration policy in the world. According to U.S. Citizenship and Immigration Services form M-1051 (12/16), there are ten steps to Naturalization. There are specific action steps under each step, but the ten steps are listed below.

Step 1 – Determine if you are already a U.S. citizen.

Step 2 – Determine your eligibility to become a U.S. citizen.

Step 3 – Prepare Form N-400, Application for Naturalization.

Step 4 – Submit Form N-400, Application for Naturalization.

Step 5 – Go to the biometrics appointment, if applicable.

Step 6 – Complete the interview.

Step 7 – Receive a decision from USCIS on your Form N-400.

Step 8 – Receive a notice to take the Oath of Allegiance.

Step 9 – Take the Oath of Allegiance to the United States.

Step 10 – Understanding U.S. citizenship.

One of the major steps in this process for future citizens is to understand the basics of what it means to be an American. The culmination of this naturalization process is taking the citizenship oath. Below is the oath for new citizens. I would guess that many Americans have never read this oath. Please read it now.

Citizenship Oath of the United States of America

I hereby declare, on oath, that I absolutely and entirely renounce and abjure all allegiance and fidelity to any foreign prince, potentate, state, or sovereignty, of whom or which I have heretofore been a subject or citizen; that I will support and defend the Constitution and laws of the United States of America against all enemies, foreign and domestic; that I will bear true faith and allegiance to the same; that I will bear arms on behalf of the United States when required by the law; that I will perform noncombatant service in the Armed Forces of the United States when required by the law; that I will perform work of national importance under civilian direction when required by the law; and that I take this obligation freely, without any mental reservation or purpose of evasion; so help me God.

It is harmful to the future of America when this assimilation process through legal immigration is avoided. Imagine if everyone in our country read and honored the citizenship oath. Enforcing our immigration laws is not hatred or racism; it is one key element of our national security and national identity. Our borders must be protected and our immigration laws must be followed in order for our country to be safe. There is a problem: our government, businesses, and the education system are incentivizing illegal behavior.

Our Media is Out of Control

To say that the news media is out of control is a gross understatement. The common topic in the media is fake news. Fake news is creating or falsely reporting a story that promotes a personal or political agenda. The amount of misinformation online and on the airways is staggering. In a perfect world, news should be a factual telling of a story. The reporting of the facts should never be filtered through any bias. Today's media has taken biased reporting to a new level. Facts are whatever the news agency, commentator, blogger, or reporter wants them to be in order to move an agenda forward. Many of these stories now fall under the category of propaganda and are creating disunity and panic in America.

The news media has an evil twin. For as long as movies and television have been broadcast, the liberal-agenda-driven entertainment industry has indoctrinated their audience with their views on government, war, sexuality, corruption, politics, family, alcohol, drug use, and violence. In the 1940s and 1950s there was massive hysteria over the threat of communism infiltrating the United States. The main focus of concern was the entertainment business. Many people in Hollywood were investigated for ties to communism and their use of this industry to promote this anti-American political system.

Today the entertainment industry continues their attack on America. The depth and breadth of this attack is massive. The attack starts with morality issues like homosexuality, gay marriage, alcohol and drug use, and the family. The attack continues with politics and policies. The two primary topics entertainers promote are climate change and big government. These attacks have been effective and would appear to be impossible to reverse.

The Story Continues

That's enough negativity. Don't feel hopeless. There is hope for America. God's Word gives us wisdom for such a time as this. The next chapter describes the biblical design for freedom. Some Americans want the government completely out of our lives. Others want the government to control everything. The Bible teaches that there can be a healthy partnership between the government and its citizens. Government shouldn't be our enemy or savior. It should only be the structure and protector of our freedom.

LIBERTY KEY 2

We Must Stand Firm in Our Freedom!

CHAPTER 5
Freedom's Design
The Biblical Model

These are the words that started it all. Please read them slowly and carefully. Some **key words** and **phrases** have been **bolded**.

The Preamble to the Declaration of Independence

When in the Course of human events, it **becomes necessary** for one people to dissolve the political bands which have connected them with another, and to assume among the powers of the earth, **the separate and equal station** to which the Laws of Nature and of Nature's God entitle them, a decent respect to the opinions of mankind requires that they should declare the causes which impel them **to the separation**.

We hold these truths to be **self-evident**, that **all men are created equal**, that **they are endowed by their Creator with certain unalienable Rights, that among these are Life, Liberty and the pursuit of Happiness.**–That **to secure these rights**, Governments are instituted among Men, **deriving their just powers from the consent of the governed, –That whenever any Form of Government becomes destructive of these ends, it is the Right of the People to alter or to abolish it, and to institute new Government, laying its foundation on such principles and organizing its powers in such form,**

as to them shall seem most likely to effect their Safety and Happiness. Prudence, indeed, will dictate that Governments long established should not be changed for light and transient causes; and accordingly all experience hath shewn, that mankind are more disposed to suffer, while evils are sufferable, than to right themselves by abolishing the forms to which they are accustomed. But when a long train of abuses and usurpations, pursuing invariably the same Object evinces a design to reduce them under absolute Despotism, **it is their right, it is their duty, to throw off such Government, and to provide new Guards for their future security.**–Such has been the patient sufferance of these Colonies; and such is now the necessity which constrains them to alter their former Systems of Government. The history of the present King of Great Britain is a history of repeated injuries and usurpations, all having in direct object the establishment of an absolute Tyranny over these States. To prove this, let Facts be submitted to a candid world.

These words are truly amazing, but, shockingly, we are repeating our history that led to the writing of these words. America is back under a similar type of tyranny endured by our pre-Revolutionary War founders. We have a new King George III. Our new king is the massive United States federal government. We have an oversized and out of control federal government. Even with the election of Donald Trump and the possibility of reducing the size of government, too few Americans find this problematic. There are two primary concerns related to our growing government and the reduction of the freedoms of American citizens. First, there is a disturbing indifference for the adherence of the rule of law in America. Even in the best of circumstances, it will be a massive undertaking to change direction and take America back to our founding principles. Without a complete respect for and adherence to the United States Constitution, this task may be impossible. Second, there is a volatile political divide in America. We are one midterm and one general election away from being back where we were prior to the 2016 election. We will stop being America when we stop doing the things that make us America. So, what are we going to do?

The great news is that we do not have to start over. All we need to do is return to what our founders created. Granted our country is an enormous mess, like a bunch of puzzle pieces in a box. The good news is that we have the picture on the box to show us how the puzzle pieces all fit back together. In many ways the decision to declare freedom from England was easy. The British soldiers were invading the colonies and killing the colonialists. The colonists had to surrender, fight, or die. Today, many of the enemies of the America as founded are our own fellow citizens and others present in our country legally or illegally. They may be our own neighbors, friends, coworkers, or even our family. They may not desire to hurt us physically, but their political philosophy and policies are directly opposed to America's founding principles. They desire an ever-growing and controlling federal government with a dependent and blindly obedient population.

There is one overarching principle that we as Christian Americans need to commit to in order to help peacefully restore America to its full potential: We need to first be obedient to the Word of God in all matters of life. Second, we must obey the laws of our country, which include the United States Constitution, state laws, and local laws.

As Christians, the Word of God is the authority over our lives. The Bible shows us what to do and how to do it. Romans 13 teaches Christian Americans the fundamental truth concerning how we are to interact with our government. As we dig deeper into the text, we will see that these seven verses contain the clearest and most specific New Testament teaching on the Christian's responsibility to civil authority.

Every person is to be in subjection to the governing authorities. For there is no authority except from God, and those which exist are established by God. Therefore whoever resists authority has opposed the ordinance of God; and they who have opposed will receive condemnation upon themselves. For rulers are not a cause of fear for good behavior, but for evil. Do you want to have no fear of authority? Do what is good and you will have praise from the same;

for it is a minister of God to you for good. But if you do what is evil, be afraid; for it does not bear the sword for nothing; for it is a minister of God, an avenger who brings wrath on the one who practices evil. Therefore it is necessary to be in subjection, not only because of wrath, but also for conscience' sake. For because of this you also pay taxes, for rulers are servants of God, devoting themselves to this very thing. Render to all what is due them: tax to whom tax is due; custom to whom custom; fear to whom fear; honor to whom honor. (Rom 13:1–7)

There are two key points in this passage. The first one is found in verse one and the second one is found in verses two through seven.

Key Point #1

(Romans 13:1)
"Every person is to be subject to the governing authorities.
For there is no authority except from God,
and those which exist are established by God."

"Every Person"

These two words are crystal clear. Every person is to be subject to the governing authorities. This simply means that all people within our borders (including every person who works for the government in any position at the local, state, or federal level and our country's guests) must be subject to the governing authority of the United States. Herman Belz agrees with this view and states in his book, *Constitutionalism and the Rule of Law in America*, "Rule of Law–government as well as the governed are subject to the law and that all are to be equally protected by the law."[1]

One of greatest harms for our free society is the belief that not all citizens are equal under the law. A second great harm for America is a belief that our elected and appointed governmental leaders are above the law. The people charged with writing, passing, and enforcing laws cannot live outside those same laws. In other words, everyone must live inside the structure created by the rule of law. No exceptions!

"Is to Be Subject to"

This phrase gives many people trouble. There are many people living within our borders who choose not to be subject to our governing authorities. They simply break our laws. Whether they are citizens, guests, or seemingly countless numbers of people who populate our prison system, many people do not consider themselves subject to anything or anybody. Being in subjection simply means to be under authority. It does not mean blind or docile conformity. People will naturally rebel against authority. This is even a challenge for Christian Americans who continue their struggle with being subject to any authority even after forgiveness of sin and surrendering to the lordship of Jesus Christ. This is a command and not an option. We are all to be subject to and under the authority of our governing authorities.

"The Governing Authorities"

Understanding this phrase is the most critical task of all. Simply defined, governing means "to hold above or to be superior." Authority means "to have the power to act." I believe that the best meaning of "governing authorities" is not simply the people in positions of authority but our legal documents that provide the structure and authority for the officials to act. A simple example is the badge a law enforcement officer wears. The power is not in the person who wears the badge but in what the badge represents. In America we are not governed by the diabolical plans of individuals or political parties. We are governed by our design, the United States Constitution. It should be very comforting to realize that the governing authorities are not the people or leaders in office but the laws created by the process established in the United States Constitution.

A dangerous understanding of governing authorities is that anyone in a position of authority can make or break the law. What is so dangerous about that view? Everything! Our entire society is established upon the principles of the rule of law; if we were to continue down that path of lawlessness our society would soon reflect the potentially deplorable values of its leadership. Our country could be trapped by the tyranny of an all-powerful leader. The best understanding to this passage is that all Americans and our guests are subject to governing authorities, which is not a person or group of leaders, but the United States Constitution.

"For there is no authority except from God, and those which exist are established by God."

In our politically correct world, the statement "for there is no authority except from God, and those which exist are established by God" brings an obvious and immediate negative reaction. Who would dare say that all authority comes from God? Too many people believe that the government has all authority. Sadly, even more believe that God, if he exists, has nothing to do with the authority of governments. The founders believed in God as the Creator. The Preamble of the Declaration of Independence declares powerfully: "that they are endowed by their Creator with certain unalienable rights, that among these are life, liberty and the pursuit of happiness." Our first founding document acknowledges that God is the source of all the rights of mankind. This great document also states that governments are established to secure these rights given to men by their Creator. The Word of God declares that God is the source of all authority. The Preamble declares that the Creator is the source of all rights. The challenge is to convince the religiously diverse world that the Word of God is the only truth and that God is indeed the source of all authority, including authority granted to governing authorities.

This phase also stimulates many questions that may be beyond the scope of this book. There is one obvious issue, however, that needs to be discussed: How can God allow the establishment of governments that govern in ways that are seemingly contrary to his word and his plans? Isaiah 55:8 reads, "For My thoughts are not your thoughts, Nor are your ways My ways,' declares the Lord." The answer to that question is simply "God's ways are not my ways." The answer is only found in the wisdom and knowledge of God. This is where faith comes into play. We have to trust God and accept his ways by faith. We have to be willing to live with the mystery that faith in God creates. We can accept that mystery because we know that he loves us. We must honor and obey him and believe that his plan for the world is beyond the scope of our understanding.

Key Point #2

(Romans 13:2-7)
Warnings and Instructions

Warnings

The Bible gives us four warnings concerning being in subjection to governing authorities. These warning are found in Romans 13: 2-4.

Warning 1: Resistance to Authority Opposes God's Ordinances

Resistance to the governing authorities, the laws of our land, is resistance to the ordinances of God. God commands us to not only obey the laws but also the authorities that represent the laws of the United States. Failure to comply with any law opposes the ordinances of God.

Warning 2: Opposition Brings Condemnation

The one who resists authority is fighting against what God has ordained. The result is condemnation. Condemnation is to pronounce judgment against someone. These are powerful words when we think about how casually people all across the land are breaking the law. God's promise of condemnation can be fulfilled within the structure of the court system, or it may not happen until that person stands before the holy God facing his judgment, but it will happen.

Warning 3: Evil Behavior Causes Fear

When the law is broken, it causes fear for the one who is guilty. No one enjoys being stopped by an officer for a traffic violation. No one wants to receive a letter from the IRS requesting an audit. Evil behavior causes fear. Caught or waiting to be caught for breaking the law causes fear in the hearts of the law breaker. Only when we live within the law does the fear stop.

Warning 4: Evil Behavior Brings Wrath

Evil behavior brings wrath is a simple yet profound truth. When accused law-breakers are found guilty, they will face the verdict of the courts. The punishment will be monetary or some type of incarceration. God delegates His wrath to governments and therefore affirms the government's use of punishment. There are also consequences beyond the power and the scope of the law. God will also bring His wrath upon those deserving punishment, whether temporal or eternal.

Instructions

The Bible gives us two instructions concerning being in subjection to governing authorities. These instructions are found in Romans 13:5-7.

Instruction 1: Be in Subjection

The passage gives two primary reasons—one internal and one external—to be in subjection to our governing authorities. We must be in subjection for the fear of or the threat of wrath. In its primary context wrath or justice comes from the legal or law enforcement representatives of the governing authorities. It is also fair to say that wrath can also come from God himself as punishment for disobedience.

The second primary reason to be in subjection to our governing authorities involves our conscience. Christ followers know that obedience to the Word of God is a primary responsibility. Deep down in our very soul, we know that we must be in subjection to our governing authorities because that is what God has commanded us to do. Our heart and mind tell us that we must obey him.

Instruction 2: Pay What You Owe

This instruction comes with two parts. We are to pay twice. Before you get angry, let me explain. First, we are to pay taxes. Our taxes support the ones in authority and provide them with what they need to effectively do their work. Taxes are the general obligation of every citizen. Pay what you owe! Second, we are to pay our due respect and honor those in authority. The list is long and includes everyone in government, from the president of the United States to the new private in our armed services. We must also honor all of our state and local officials and our police. Honor someone today!

The Story Continues

Having defined governing authorities and reviewed what the Word of God says about how Christ followers must be in subjection to their governing authorities, it is now time to see the American design of freedom. The United States Constitution is one of the finest, if not the finest, political documents ever written. It not only lays out the design for how Americans are to self-govern, but it also gives us the instructions for how to change the document. Americans and our guests enjoy the peace and prosperity that the founders provided through their arduous work to write of our constitution. What they accomplished allowed future generations of Americans to live in the greatest country in history. Enjoy your review of this fabulous document.

CHAPTER 6
Freedom's Design
The American Model

In America, liberty is more than just a slogan; it is in our DNA. Our freedom began to take root with the echoes of these words that are attributed to James Otis in 1761: "No taxation without representation." This phrase developed from another phrase that stated "Taxation without representation is tyranny." As you may remember, this was the chief complaint about the British Parliament in their treatment of the American colonies. These words remind us of a powerful truth about America. We are a representative republic, not a democracy with majority rule. Matthew Spalding in his book, *We Still Hold These Truths*, states, "The Founders sought to correct the historic problem of majority tyranny while remaining true to the principle of popular government."[1] Spalding continues, "The solution of the men who wrote the Constitution, famously laid out in *The Federalist*, was to control the political effects of these differences and thwart the formation of unjust majorities while celebrating the natural diversity inherent in human liberty."[2]

This important distinction was once again revealed in the 2016 presidential election regarding the Electoral College. The function of the Electoral College is found in the United States Constitution in Article 2, Section 1 and in the Twelfth Amendment. Many in the party that lost the election called for the dismantling of the Electoral College. The value of the Electoral College is a perfect reason why America was designed as a representative republic rather than a true democracy by majority rule. In short, this distinction is critical because it allows the votes of all the citizens from each state to have equal value in the presidential election. It also gives each state a proportionate number of representatives in Congress. This is important because the government protects the rights of all citizens and not just the majority that may be found in a minority of states.

America is the greatest nation in the history of the world for two reasons: our people and our system of government as designed by the founders. The United States of America is a sovereign nation and requires structure to function properly. Our structure is the United States Constitution. Susan Dunn writes concerning the United States Constitution in her book, *Sister Revolutions*, "The achievement of the founders is breathtaking."[3] Gerard Bradley said in his book *Religious Liberty in the American Republic*, "The United States Constitution is almost entirely about government superstructure."[4] Bradley continued, "First, the Constitution obviously establishes a federal system in which the national government has limited, enumerated powers. This is the reserve of the states. The state constitutions set up governments with authority to legislate on family structure, religion, education, public morals—all the glue that holds civil society together."[5] Mark Levin stated in his book, *Liberty and Tyranny*, that "The Constitution is the bedrock on which a living, evolving nation was built. It is—and must be—a timeless yet durable foundation that individuals can count on in a changing world."[6]

Other historians and writers have this to say about the United States Constitution:

> The challenge for the American Founders in framing the Constitution was to secure the rights and liberties promised in the Declaration of Independence, preserving a republican form of government that reflected

the consent of the governed yet avoided despotism and tyranny.[7]

The Declaration of Independence assets unalienable rights to "life, liberty, and the pursuit of happiness," and the Constitution is meant to "secure the blessings of liberty."[8]

The creation of the United States Constitution—John Adams described the Constitutional Convention as "the greatest single effort of national deliberation that the world has ever seen"—was one of the greatest events in the history of human liberty.[9]

The Constitution transformed the revolutionary principles of federalism and republicanism into a system of national authority.[10]

The kind of government proposed by the framers of our Constitution was intended to serve the people.[11]

The History of the Design

Below is a list of events that preceded the ratification of the United States Constitution on June 21, 1788.

March 1, 1781—Articles of Confederation

The Articles created a confederation of states with a weak federal government with representatives from each state. Matthew Spalding in his book, *We Still Hold These Truths*, says this about the Articles of Confederation: "Proposed in 1777 and ratified in 1781, the Articles of Confederation are an important bridge between the government of the Continental Congress and that of the current United States Constitution."[12] On this date the Articles of Confederation were finally ratified by the thirteen states.

September 3, 1783—Treaty of Paris

The Treaty of Paris officially ended the Revolutionary War on November 25, 1783.

After more than eight years of fighting, the war officially ended with the signing of the Treaty of Paris on September 3, 1783. The war was expensive in both life and property. It created legendary heroes and infamous villains in the battle to secure liberty for the United States of America.

May 25–September 17, 1787—Constitutional Convention

The Constitutional Convention, "one of the most remarkable bodies ever assembled,"[13] met in Independence Hall in Philadelphia. James Gains, states in his book, *For Liberty and Glory*, that ". . . nobody ever delegated to the task of rethinking government had every been better prepared than the ones who gathered in Philadelphia in May of 1787."[14] The first item of business was to choose George Washington as the body's president. James Madison played a key role in the writing of the Constitution.

September 17, 1787—The Signing of United States Constitution

The Second Continental Congress agreed to pass the Constitution on to the thirteen states for ratification. The entire process lasted from December 7, 1787, to May 29, 1790. On June 21, 1788, after the ninth state, New Hampshire, ratified it, Congress passed a resolution to make the new constitution effective.

March 4, 1789—Effective Date of the United States Constitution

The United States Constitution went into effect and the Second Continental Congress disbanded and was replaced with the United States

Congress as designed in the United States Constitution.

December 15, 1791—Bill of Rights

On September 25, 1789, the United States Congress passed twelve amendments to the United States Constitution and forwarded them to the states for ratification. Only ten of the twelve Amendments were ratified with a two-thirds majority. These first ten amendments to the United States Constitution became known as the Bill of Rights. The passing of the Bill of Right is seen as a victory of states' rights because these amendments restrict the power of the federal government.

The Design

Being familiar with our founding documents will greatly assist citizens and guests in living within the rule of law. America's design is the United States Constitution. Below is the full manuscript of the United States Constitution. Please read it. Please use it as your handbook for being an American.

The United States Constitution

Preamble

We the People of the United States, in Order to form a more perfect Union, establish Justice, insure domestic Tranquility, provide for the common defence, promote the general Welfare, and secure the Blessings of Liberty to ourselves and our Posterity, do ordain and establish this Constitution for the United States of America.

Article 1 – The Legislative Branch

Section 1 – The Legislature

All legislative Powers herein granted shall be vested in a Congress of the United States, which shall consist of a Senate and House of Representatives.

Section 2 – The House

The House of Representatives shall be composed of Members chosen every second Year by the People of the several States, and the Electors in each State shall have the Qualifications requisite for Electors of the most numerous Branch of the State Legislature.

No Person shall be a Representative who shall not have attained to the Age of twenty five Years, and been seven Years a Citizen of the United States, and who shall not, when elected, be an Inhabitant of that State in which he shall be chosen.

Representatives and direct Taxes shall be apportioned among the several States which may be included within this Union, according to their respective Numbers, which shall be determined by adding to the whole Number of free Persons, including those bound to Service for a Term of Years, and excluding Indians not taxed, three fifths of all other Persons. The actual Enumeration shall be made within three Years after the first Meeting of the Congress of the United States, and within every subsequent Term of ten Years, in such Manner as they shall by Law direct. The Number of Representatives shall not exceed one for every thirty Thousand, but each State shall have at Least one Representative; and until such enumeration shall be made, the State of New Hampshire shall be entitled to choose three, Massachusetts eight, Rhode Island and Providence Plantations one, Connecticut five, New York six, New Jersey four, Pennsylvania eight,

Delaware one, Maryland six, Virginia ten, North Carolina five, South Carolina five and Georgia three.

When vacancies happen in the Representation from any State, the Executive Authority thereof shall issue Writs of Election to fill such Vacancies.

The House of Representatives shall choose their Speaker and other Officers; and shall have the sole Power of Impeachment.

Section 3 – The Senate

The Senate of the United States shall be composed of two Senators from each State, chosen by the Legislature thereof, for six Years; and each Senator shall have one Vote.

Immediately after they shall be assembled in Consequence of the first Election, they shall be divided as equally as may be into three Classes. The Seats of the Senators of the first Class shall be vacated at the Expiration of the second Year, of the second Class at the Expiration of the fourth Year, and of the third Class at the Expiration of the sixth Year, so that one third may be chosen every second Year; and if Vacancies happen by Resignation, or otherwise, during the Recess of the Legislature of any State, the Executive thereof may make temporary Appointments until the next Meeting of the Legislature, which shall then fill such Vacancies.

No person shall be a Senator who shall not have attained to the Age of thirty Years, and been nine Years a Citizen of the United States, and who shall not, when elected, be an Inhabitant of that State for which he shall be chosen.

The Vice President of the United States shall be President of the Senate, but shall have no Vote, unless they be equally divided.

The Senate shall chuse their other Officers, and also a President pro tempore, in the Absence of the Vice President, or when he shall exercise the Office of President of the United States.

The Senate shall have the sole Power to try all Impeachments. When sitting for that Purpose, they shall be on Oath or Affirmation. When the President of the United States is tried, the Chief Justice shall preside: And no Person shall be convicted without the Concurrence of two thirds of the Members present.

Judgment in Cases of Impeachment shall not extend further than to removal from Office, and disqualification to hold and enjoy any Office of honor, Trust or Profit under the United States: but the Party convicted shall nevertheless be liable and subject to indictment, Trial, Judgment and Punishment, according to Law.

Section 4 – Elections, Meetings

The Times, Places and Manner of holding Elections for Senators and Representatives, shall be prescribed in each State by the Legislature thereof; but the Congress may at any time by Law make or alter such Regulations, except as to the Place of Choosing Senators.

The Congress shall assemble at least once in every Year, and such Meeting shall be on the first Monday in December, unless they shall by Law appoint a different Day.

Section 5 – Membership, Rules, Journals, Adjournment

Each House shall be the Judge of the Elections, Returns and Qualifications of its own Members, and a Majority of each shall constitute a Quorum to do Business; but a smaller number may adjourn from day to day, and may be authorized to compel the Attendance of absent Members, in such Manner, and under such Penalties as each House may provide.

Each House may determine the Rules of its Proceedings, punish its Members for disorderly Behavior, and, with the Concurrence of two-thirds, expel a Member.

Each House shall keep a Journal of its Proceedings, and from time to time publish the same, excepting such Parts as may in their Judgment require Secrecy; and the Yeas and Nays of the Members of either House on any question shall, at the Desire of one fifth of those Present, be entered on the Journal.

Neither House, during the Session of Congress, shall, without the Consent of the other, adjourn for more than three days, nor to any other Place than that in which the two Houses shall be sitting.

Section 6 - Compensation

The Senators and Representatives shall receive a Compensation for their Services, to be ascertained by Law, and paid out of the Treasury of the United States. They shall in all Cases, except Treason, Felony and Breach of the Peace, be privileged from Arrest during their Attendance at the Session of their respective Houses, and in going to and returning from the same; and for any Speech or Debate in either House, they shall not be questioned in any other Place.

No Senator or Representative shall, during the Time for which he was elected, be appointed to any civil Office under the Authority of the United States which shall have been created, or the Emoluments whereof shall have been increased during such time; and no Person holding any Office under the United States, shall be a Member of either House during his Continuance in Office.

Section 7 – Revenue Bills, Legislative Process, Presidential Veto

All bills for raising Revenue shall originate in the House of Representatives; but the Senate may propose or concur with Amendments as on other Bills.

Every Bill which shall have passed the House of Representatives and the Senate, shall, before it become a Law, be presented to the President of the United States; If he approve he shall sign it, but if not he shall return it, with his Objections to that House in which it shall have originated, who shall enter the Objections at large on their Journal, and proceed to reconsider it. If after such Reconsideration two thirds of that House shall agree to pass the Bill, it shall be sent, together with the Objections, to the other House, by which it shall likewise be reconsidered, and if approved by two thirds of that House, it shall become a Law. But in all such Cases the Votes of both Houses shall be determined by yeas and Nays, and the Names of the Persons voting for and against the Bill shall be entered on the Journal of each House respectively. If any Bill shall not be returned by the President within ten Days (Sundays excepted) after it shall have been presented to him, the Same shall be a Law, in like Manner as if he had signed it, unless the Congress by their Adjournment prevent its Return, in which Case it shall not be a Law.

Every Order, Resolution, or Vote to which the Concurrence of the Senate and House of Representatives may be necessary (except on a question of Adjournment) shall be presented to the President of the United States; and before the Same shall take Effect, shall be approved by him, or being disapproved by him, shall be repassed by two thirds of the Senate and House of Representatives, according to the Rules and Limitations pre-scribed in the Case of a Bill.

Section 8 – Powers of Congress

The Congress shall have Power To lay and collect Taxes, Duties, Imposts and Excises, to pay the Debts and provide for the common Defence and general Welfare of the United States; but all Duties, Imposts and Excises shall be uniform throughout the United States;

To borrow money on the credit of the United States;

To regulate Commerce with foreign Nations, and among the several States, and with the Indian Tribes;

To establish an uniform Rule of Naturalization, and uniform Laws on the subject of Bankruptcies throughout the United States;

To coin Money, regulate the Value thereof, and of foreign Coin, and fix the Standard of Weights and Measures;

To provide for the Punishment of counterfeiting the Securities and current Coin of the United States;

To establish Post Offices and Post Roads;

To promote the Progress of Science and useful Arts, by securing for limited Times to Authors and Inventors the exclusive Right to their respective Writings and Discoveries;

To constitute Tribunals inferior to the supreme Court;

To define and punish Piracies and Felonies committed on the high Seas, and Offenses against the Law of Nations;

To declare War, grant Letters of Marque and Reprisal, and make Rules concerning Captures on Land and Water;

To raise and support Armies, but no Appropriation of Money to that Use shall be for a longer Term than two Years;

To provide and maintain a Navy;

To make Rules for the Government and Regulation of the land and naval Forces;

To provide for calling forth the Militia to execute the Laws of the Union, suppress Insurrections and repel Invasions;

To provide for organizing, arming, and disciplining, the Militia, and for governing such Part of them as may be employed in the Service of the

United States, reserving to the States respectively, the Appointment of the Officers, and the Authority of training the Militia according to the discipline prescribed by Congress;

To exercise exclusive Legislation in all Cases whatsoever, over such District (not exceeding ten Miles square) as may, by Cession of particular States, and the Acceptance of Congress, become the Seat of the Government of the United States, and to exercise like Authority over all Places purchased by the Consent of the Legislature of the State in which the Same shall be, for the Erection of Forts, Magazines, Arsenals, dock-Yards, and other needful Buildings; - And

To make all Laws which shall be necessary and proper for carrying into Execution the foregoing Powers, and all other Powers vested by this Constitution in the Government of the United States, or in any Department or Officer thereof.

Section 9 - Limits on Congress

The Migration or Importation of such Persons as any of the States now existing shall think proper to admit, shall not be prohibited by the Congress prior to the Year one thousand eight hundred and eight, but a Tax or duty may be imposed on such Importation, not exceeding ten dollars for each Person.

The Privilege of the Writ of Habeas Corpus shall not be suspended, unless when in Cases of Rebellion or Invasion the public Safety may require it.

No Bill of Attainder or ex post facto Law shall be passed.

No Capitation, or other direct, Tax shall be laid, unless in Proportion to the Census or enumeration herein before directed to be taken.

No Tax or Duty shall be laid on Articles exported from any State.

No Preference shall be given by any Regulation of Commerce or Revenue to the Ports of one State over those of another: nor shall Vessels bound to, or from, one State, be obliged to enter, clear, or pay Duties in another. No Money shall be drawn from the Treasury, but in Consequence of Appropriations made by Law; and a regular Statement and Account of the Receipts and Expenditures of all public Money shall be published from time to time.

No Title of Nobility shall be granted by the United States: And no Person holding any Office of Profit or Trust under them, shall, without the Consent of the Congress, accept of any present, Emolument, Office, or Title, of any kind whatever, from any King, Prince, or foreign State.

Section 10 – Powers prohibited of States

No State shall enter into any Treaty, Alliance, or Confederation; grant Letters of Marque and Reprisal; coin Money; emit Bills of Credit; make any Thing but gold and silver Coin a Tender in Payment of Debts; pass any Bill of Attainder, ex post facto Law, or Law impairing the Obligation of Contracts, or grant any Title of Nobility.

No State shall, without the Consent of the Congress, lay any Imposts or Duties on Imports or Exports, except what may be absolutely necessary for executing its inspection Laws: and the net Produce of all Duties and Imposts, laid by any State on Imports or Exports, shall be for the Use of the Treasury of the United States; and all such Laws shall be subject to the Revision and Controul of the Congress.

No State shall, without the Consent of Congress, lay any duty of Tonnage, keep Troops, or Ships of War in time of Peace, enter into any Agreement or Compact with another State, or with a foreign Power, or engage in War, unless actually invaded, or in such imminent Danger as will not admit of delay.

Article 2 – The Executive Branch

Section 1 – The President

The executive Power shall be vested in a President of the United States of America. He shall hold his Office during the Term of four Years, and, together with the Vice-President, chosen for the same Term, be elected, as follows:

Each State shall appoint, in such Manner as the Legislature thereof may direct, a Number of Electors, equal to the whole Number of Senators and Representatives to which the State may be entitled in the Congress: but no Senator or Representative, or Person holding an Office of Trust or Profit under the United States, shall be appointed an Elector.

The Electors shall meet in their respective States, and vote by Ballot for two persons, of whom one at least shall not be an Inhabitant of the same State with themselves. And they shall make a List of all the Persons voted for, and of the Number of Votes for each; which List they shall sign and certify, and transmit sealed to the Seat of the Government of the United States, directed to the President of the Senate. The President of the Senate shall, in the Presence of the Senate and House of Representatives, open all the Certificates, and the Votes shall then be counted. The Person having the greatest Number of Votes shall be the President, if such Number be a Majority of the whole Number of Electors appointed; and if there be more than one who have such Majority, and have an equal Number of Votes, then the House of Representatives shall immediately chuse by Ballot one of them for President; and if no Person have a Majority, then from the five highest on the List the said House shall in like Manner chuse the President. But in chusing the President, the Votes shall be taken by States, the Representation from each State having one Vote; a quorum

for this purpose shall consist of a Member or Members from two thirds of the States, and a Majority of all the States shall be necessary to a Choice. In every Case, after the Choice of the President, the Person having the greatest Number of Votes of the Electors shall be the Vice President. But if there should remain two or more who have equal Votes, the Senate shall chuse from them by Ballot the Vice-President.

The Congress may determine the Time of chusing the Electors, and the Day on which they shall give their Votes; which Day shall be the same throughout the United States.

No person except a natural born Citizen, or a Citizen of the United States, at the time of the Adoption of this Constitution, shall be eligible to the Office of President; neither shall any Person be eligible to that Office who shall not have attained to the Age of thirty-five Years, and been fourteen Years a Resident within the United States.

In Case of the Removal of the President from Office, or of his Death, Resignation, or Inability to discharge the Powers and Duties of the said Office, the Same shall devolve on the Vice President, and the Congress may by Law provide for the Case of Removal, Death, Resignation or Inability, both of the President and Vice President, declaring what Officer shall then act as President, and such Officer shall act accordingly, until the Disability be removed, or a President shall be elected.

The President shall, at stated Times, receive for his Services, a Compensation, which shall neither be increased nor diminished during the Period for which he shall have been elected, and he shall not receive within that Period any other Emolument from the United States, or any of them.

Before he enter on the Execution of his Office, he shall take the following Oath or Affirmation: - "I do solemnly swear (or affirm) that I will faithfully execute the Office of President of the United States, and will to the best of my Ability, preserve, protect and defend the Constitution of the United States."

Section 2 – Civilian Power over Military, Cabinet, Pardon Power, Appointments

The President shall be Commander in Chief of the Army and Navy of the United States, and of the Militia of the several States, when called into the actual Service of the United States; he may require the Opinion, in writing, of the principal Officer in each of the executive Departments, upon any subject relating to the Duties of their respective Offices, and he shall have Power to grant Reprieves and Pardons for Offenses against the United States, except in Cases of Impeachment.

He shall have Power, by and with the Advice and Consent of the Senate, to make Treaties, provided two thirds of the Senators present concur; and he shall nominate, and by and with the Advice and Consent of the Senate, shall appoint Ambassadors, other public Ministers and Consuls, Judges of the supreme Court, and all other Officers of the United States, whose Appointments are not herein otherwise provided for, and which shall be established by Law: but the Congress may by Law vest the Appointment of such inferior Officers, as they think proper, in the President alone, in the Courts of Law, or in the Heads of Departments.

The President shall have Power to fill up all Vacancies that may happen during the Recess of the Senate, by granting Commissions which shall expire at the End of their next Session.

Section 3 – State of the Union, Convening Congress

He shall from time to time give to the Congress Information of the State of the Union, and recommend to their Consideration such Measures as he shall judge necessary and expedient; he may, on extraordinary Occasions, convene both Houses, or either of them, and in Case of Disagreement between them, with Respect to the Time of Adjournment, he may adjourn them to such Time as he shall think proper; he shall receive Ambassadors and other public Ministers; he shall take Care that the Laws be faithfully executed, and shall Commission all the Officers of the United States.

Section 4 - Disqualification

The President, Vice President and all civil Officers of the United States, shall be removed from Office on Impeachment for, and Conviction of, Treason, Bribery, or other high Crimes and Misdemeanors.

Article 3 - The Judicial Branch

Section 1 - Judicial Powers

The judicial Power of the United States, shall be vested in one supreme Court, and in such inferior Courts as the Congress may from time to time ordain and establish. The Judges, both of the supreme and inferior Courts, shall hold their Offices during good Behaviour, and shall, at stated Times, receive for their Services a Compensation which shall not be diminished during their Continuance in Office.

Section 2 - Trial by Jury, Original Jurisdiction, Jury Trials

The judicial Power shall extend to all Cases, in Law and Equity, arising under this Constitution, the Laws of the United States, and Treaties made, or which shall be made, under their Authority; - to all Cases affecting Ambassadors, other public Ministers and Consuls; - to all Cases of admiralty and maritime Jurisdiction; - to Controversies to which the United States shall be a Party; - to Controversies between two or more States; - between a State and Citizens of another State; between Citizens of different States; - between Citizens of the same State claiming Lands under

Grants of different States, and between a State, or the Citizens thereof, and foreign States, Citizens or Subjects.

In all Cases affecting Ambassadors, other public Ministers and Consuls, and those in which a State shall be Party, the supreme Court shall have original Jurisdiction. In all the other Cases before mentioned, the supreme Court shall have appellate Jurisdiction, both as to Law and Fact, with such Exceptions, and under such Regulations as the Congress shall make.

The Trial of all Crimes, except in Cases of Impeachment, shall be by Jury; and such Trial shall be held in the State where the said Crimes shall have been committed; but when not committed within any State, the Trial shall be at such Place or Places as the Congress may by Law have directed.

Section 3 - Treason

Treason against the United States, shall consist only in levying War against them, or in adhering to their Enemies, giving them Aid and Comfort. No Person shall be convicted of Treason unless on the Testimony of two Witnesses to the same overt Act, or on Confession in open Court.

The Congress shall have power to declare the Punishment of Treason, but no Attainder of Treason shall work Corruption of Blood, or Forfeiture except during the Life of the Person attainted.

Article 4 – The States

Section 1 – Each State to Honor all others

Full Faith and Credit shall be given in each State to the public Acts, Records, and judicial Proceedings of every other State. And the Congress may by general Laws prescribe the Manner in which such Acts, Records and Proceedings shall be proved, and the Effect thereof.

Section 2 – State citizens, Extradition

The Citizens of each State shall be entitled to all Privileges and Immunities of Citizens in the several States.

A Person charged in any State with Treason, Felony, or other Crime, who shall flee from Justice, and be found in another State, shall on Demand of the executive Authority of the State from which he fled, be delivered up, to be removed to the State having Jurisdiction of the Crime.

No Person held to Service or Labour in one State, under the Laws thereof, escaping into another, shall, in Consequence of any Law or Regulation therein, be discharged from such Service or Labour, but shall be delivered up on Claim of the Party to whom such Service or Labour may be due.

Section 3 – New States

New States may be admitted by the Congress into this Union; but no new States shall be formed or erected within the Jurisdiction of any other State; nor any State be formed by the Junction of two or more States, or Parts of States, without the Consent of the Legislatures of the States concerned as well as of the Congress.

The Congress shall have Power to dispose of and make all needful Rules and Regulations respecting the Territory or other Property belonging to the United States; and nothing in this Constitution shall be so construed as to Prejudice any Claims of the United States, or of any particular State.

Section 4 – Republican government

The United States shall guarantee to every State in this Union a Republican Form of Government, and shall protect each of them against Invasion; and on Application of the Legislature, or of the Executive (when the Legislature cannot be convened), against domestic Violence.

Article 5 - Amendment

The Congress, whenever two thirds of both Houses shall deem it necessary, shall propose Amendments to this Constitution, or, on the Application of the Legislatures of two thirds of the several States, shall call a Convention for proposing Amendments, which, in either Case, shall be valid to all Intents and Purposes, as part of this Constitution, when ratified by the Legislatures of three fourths of the several States, or by Conventions in three fourths thereof, as the one or the other Mode of Ratification may be proposed by the Congress; Provided that no Amendment which may be made prior to the Year One thousand eight hundred and eight shall in any Manner affect the first and fourth Clauses in the Ninth Section of the first Article; and that no State, without its Consent, shall be deprived of its equal Suffrage in the Senate.

Article 6 - Debts, Supremacy, Oaths

All Debts contracted and Engagements entered into, before the Adoption of this Constitution, shall be as valid against the United States under this Constitution, as under the Confederation.

This Constitution, and the Laws of the United States which shall be made in Pursuance thereof; and all Treaties made, or which shall be made, under the Authority of the United States, shall be the supreme Law of the Land; and the Judges in every State shall be bound thereby, any Thing in the Constitution or Laws of any State to the Contrary notwithstanding.

The Senators and Representatives before mentioned, and the Members of the several State Legislatures, and all executive and judicial Officers, both of the United States and of the several States, shall be bound by Oath or Affirmation, to support this Constitution; but no religious Test shall ever be required as a Qualification to any Office or public Trust under the

United States.

Article 7 - Ratification

The Ratification of the Conventions of nine States, shall be sufficient for the Establishment of this Constitution between the States so ratifying the Same. Done in Convention by the Unanimous Consent of the States present the Seventeenth Day of September in the Year of our Lord one thousand seven hundred and Eighty seven and of the Independence of the United States of America the Twelfth. In Witness whereof We have hereunto subscribed our Names.

George Washington - President and deputy from Virginia

New Hampshire - John Langdon, Nicholas Gilman

Massachusetts - Nathaniel Gorham, Rufus King

Connecticut - William Samuel Johnson, Roger Sherman

New York - Alexander Hamilton

New Jersey - William Livingston, David Brearley, William Paterson, Jonathan Dayton

Pennsylvania - Benjamin Franklin, Thomas Mifflin, Robert Morris, George Clymer, Thomas Fitzsimons, Jared Ingersoll, James Wilson, Gouvernour Morris

Delaware - George Read, Gunning Bedford Jr., John Dickinson, Richard Bassett, Jacob Broom

Maryland - James McHenry, Daniel of St Thomas Jenifer, Daniel Carroll

Virginia - John Blair, James Madison Jr.

North Carolina - William Blount, Richard Dobbs Spaight, Hugh Williamson

South Carolina - John Rutledge, Charles Cotesworth Pinckney, Charles Pinckney, Pierce Butler

Georgia - William Few, Abraham Baldwin

Attest: William Jackson, Secretary

The Amendments
(The first ten are known as the Bill of Rights)

Amendment 1 - Freedom of Religion, Press, Expression

Congress shall make no law respecting an establishment of religion, or prohibiting the free exercise thereof; or abridging the freedom of speech, or of the press; or the right of the people peaceably to assemble, and to petition the Government for a redress of grievances.
Ratified 12/15/1791

Amendment 2 - Right to Bear Arms

A well regulated Militia, being necessary to the security of a free State, the right of the people to keep and bear Arms, shall not be infringed. **Ratified 12/15/1791**

Amendment 3 - Quartering of Soldiers

No Soldier shall, in time of peace be quartered in any house, without the consent of the Owner, nor in time of war, but in a manner to be prescribed by law.
Ratified 12/15/1791

Amendment 4 - Search and Seizure

The right of the people to be secure in their persons, houses, papers, and effects, against unreasonable searches and seizures, shall not be violated, and no Warrants shall issue, but upon probable cause, supported by Oath or affirmation, and particularly describing the place to be searched, and the persons or things to be seized.

Ratified 12/15/1791

Amendment 5 – Trial and Punishment, Compensation for Taking

No person shall be held to answer for a capital, or otherwise infamous crime, unless on a presentment or indictment of a Grand Jury, except in cases arising in the land or naval forces, or in the Militia, when in actual service in time of War or public danger; nor shall any person be subject for the same offense to be twice put in jeopardy of life or limb; nor shall be compelled in any criminal case to be a witness against himself, nor be deprived of life, liberty, or property, without due process of law; nor shall private property be taken for public use, without just compensation.

Ratified 12/15/1791

Amendment 6 – Right to Speedy Trial, Confrontation of Witnesses

In all criminal prosecutions, the accused shall enjoy the right to a speedy and public trial, by an impartial jury of the State and district wherein the crime shall have been committed, which district shall have been previously ascertained by law, and to be informed of the nature and cause of the accusation; to be confronted with the witnesses against him; to have compulsory process for obtaining witnesses in his favor, and to have the Assistance of Counsel for his defence.

Ratified 12/15/1791

Amendment 7 – Trial by Jury in Civil Cases

In Suits at common law, where the value in controversy shall exceed twenty dollars, the right of trial by jury shall be preserved, and no fact tried by a jury, shall be otherwise re-examined in any Court of the United States, than according to the rules of the common law.

Ratified 12/15/1791

Amendment 8 - Cruel and Unusual Punishment

Excessive bail shall not be required, nor excessive fines imposed, nor cruel and unusual punishments inflicted.

Ratified 12/15/1791

Amendment 9 - Construction of Constitution

The enumeration in the Constitution, of certain rights, shall not be construed to deny or disparage others retained by the people.

Ratified 12/15/1791

Amendment 10 - Powers of the States and People

The powers not delegated to the United States by the Constitution, nor prohibited by it to the States, are reserved to the States respectively, or to the people.

Ratified 12/15/1791

Amendment 11 - Judicial Limits

The Judicial power of the United States shall not be construed to extend to any suit in law or equity, commenced or prosecuted against one of the United States by Citizens of another State, or by Citizens or Subjects of any Foreign State.

Ratified 2/7/1795

Amendment 12 - Choosing the President, Vice-President

The Electors shall meet in their respective states, and vote by ballot for President and Vice-President, one of whom, at least, shall not be an inhabitant of the same state with themselves; they shall name in their ballots the person voted for as President, and in distinct ballots the person voted for as Vice-President, and they shall make distinct lists of all persons voted for as President, and of all persons voted for as Vice-President and of the number of votes for each, which lists they shall sign and certify, and transmit sealed to the seat of the government of the United States, directed to the President of the Senate; - the President of the Senate shall, in the presence of the Senate and House of Representatives, open all the certificates and the votes shall then be counted; - The person having the greatest number of votes for President, shall be the President, if such number be a majority of the whole number of Electors appointed; and if no person have such majority, then from the persons having the highest numbers not exceeding three on the list of those voted for as President, the House of Representatives shall choose immediately, by ballot, the President. But in choosing the President, the votes shall be taken by states, the representation from each state having one vote; a quorum for this purpose shall consist of a member or members from two-thirds of the states, and a majority of all the states shall be necessary to a choice. (And if the House of Representatives shall not choose a President whenever the right of choice shall devolve upon them, before the fourth day of March next following, then the Vice-President shall act as President, as in the case of the death or other constitutional disability of the President.) The person having the greatest number of votes as Vice-President, shall be the Vice-President, if such number be a majority of the whole number of Electors appointed, and if no person have a majority, then from the two highest numbers on the list, the Senate shall choose the Vice-President; a quorum for the purpose shall consist of two-thirds of the whole number of Senators, and a majority of the whole number shall be necessary to a choice. But no person constitutionally ineligible to the office of President shall be eligible to that of Vice-President of the United States.

Ratified 6/15/1804

Amendment 13 – Slavery Abolished

Section1

Neither slavery nor involuntary servitude, except as a punishment for crime whereof the party shall have been duly convicted, shall exist within the United States, or any place subject to their jurisdiction.

Section 2

Congress shall have power to enforce this article by appropriate legislation.

Ratified 12/6/1865

Amendment 14 – Citizenship Rights

Section 1

All persons born or naturalized in the United States, and subject to the jurisdiction thereof, are citizens of the United States and of the State wherein they reside. No State shall make or enforce any law which shall abridge the privileges or immunities of citizens of the United States; nor shall any State deprive any person of life, liberty, or property, without due process of law; nor deny to any person within its jurisdiction the equal protection of the laws.

Section 2

Representatives shall be apportioned among the several States according to their respective numbers, counting the whole number of persons in each State, excluding Indians not taxed. But when the right to vote at any election for the choice of electors for President and Vice-President of the United States, Representatives in Congress, the Executive and Judicial officers of a State, or the members of the Legislature thereof, is denied to any of the male inhabitants of such State, being twenty-one years of age, and citizens of the United States, or in any way abridged, except for participation in rebellion, or other crime, the basis of representation therein shall be reduced in the proportion which the number of such male citizens shall bear to the whole number of male citizens twenty-one years of age in such State.

Section 3

No person shall be a Senator or Representative in Congress, or elector of President and Vice-President, or hold any office, civil or military, under the United States, or under any State, who, having previously taken an oath, as a member of Congress, or as an officer of the United States, or as a member of any State legislature, or as an executive or judicial officer of any State, to support the Constitution of the United States, shall have engaged in insurrection or rebellion against the same, or given aid or comfort to the enemies thereof. But Congress may by a vote of two-thirds of each House, remove such disability.

Section 4

The validity of the public debt of the United States, authorized by law, including debts incurred for payment of pensions and bounties for services in suppressing insurrection or rebellion, shall not be questioned. But neither the United States nor any State shall assume or pay any debt or obligation incurred in aid of insurrection or rebellion against the United States, or any claim for the loss or emancipation of any slave; but all such debts, obligations and claims shall be held illegal and void.

Section 5

The Congress shall have power to enforce, by appropriate legislation, the provisions of this article.

Ratified 7/9/1868

Amendment 15 – Race No Bar to Vote

Section 1

The right of citizens of the United States to vote shall not be denied or abridged by the United States or by any State on account of race, color, or previous condition of servitude.

Section 2

The Congress shall have power to enforce this article by appropriate legislation.

Ratified 2/3/1870

Amendment 16 – Status of Income Tax Clarified

The Congress shall have power to lay and collect taxes on incomes, from whatever source derived, without apportionment among the several States, and without regard to any census or enumeration.

Ratified 2/3/1913

Amendment 17 – Senators Elected by Popular Vote

The Senate of the United States shall be composed of two Senators from each State, elected by the people thereof, for six years; and each Senator shall have one vote. The electors in each State shall have the qualifications requisite for electors of the most numerous branch of the State legislatures. When vacancies happen in the representation of any State in the Senate, the executive authority of such State shall issue writs of election to fill such vacancies: Provided, That the legislature of any State may empower the executive thereof to make temporary appointments until the people fill the vacancies by election as the legislature may direct.

This amendment shall not be so construed as to affect the election or term of any Senator chosen before it becomes valid as part of the Constitution.

Ratified 4/8/1913

Amendment 18 – Liquor Abolished

Section 1

After one year from the ratification of this article the manufacture, sale, or transportation of intoxicating liquors within, the importation thereof into, or the exportation thereof from the United States and all territory subject to the jurisdiction thereof for beverage purposes is hereby prohibited.

Section 2

The Congress and the several States shall have concurrent power to enforce this article by appropriate legislation.

Section 3

This article shall be inoperative unless it shall have been ratified as an amendment to the Constitution by the legislatures of the several States, as provided in the Constitution, within seven years from the date of the submission hereof to the States by the Congress.

Ratified 1/16/1919

Amendment 19 – Women's Suffrage

The right of citizens of the United States to vote shall not be denied or abridged by the United States or by any State on account of sex.

Congress shall have power to enforce this article by appropriate legislation.

Ratified 8/18/1920

Amendment 20 – Presidential, Congressional Terms

Section 1

The terms of the President and Vice President shall end at noon on the 20th day of January, and the terms of Senators and Representatives at noon on the 3d day of January, of the years in which such terms would have ended if this article had not been ratified; and the terms of their successors shall then begin.

Section 2

The Congress shall assemble at least once in every year, and such meeting shall begin at noon on the 3d day of January, unless they shall by law appoint a different day.

Section 3

If, at the time fixed for the beginning of the term of the President, the

President elect shall have died, the Vice President elect shall become President. If a President shall not have been chosen before the time fixed for the beginning of his term, or if the President elect shall have failed to qualify, then the Vice President elect shall act as President until a President shall have qualified; and the Congress may by law provide for the case wherein neither a President elect nor a Vice President elect shall have qualified, declaring who shall then act as President, or the manner in which one who is to act shall be selected, and such person shall act accordingly until a President or Vice President shall have qualified.

Section 4

The Congress may by law provide for the case of the death of any of the persons from whom the House of Representatives may choose a President whenever the right of choice shall have devolved upon them, and for the case of the death of any of the persons from whom the Senate may choose a Vice President whenever the right of choice shall have devolved upon them.

Section 5

Sections 1 and 2 shall take effect on the 15th day of October following the ratification of this article.

Section 6

This article shall be inoperative unless it shall have been ratified as an amendment to the Constitution by the legislatures of three-fourths of the several States within seven years from the date of its submission.

Ratified 1/23/1933

Amendment 21 – Amendment 18 Repealed

Section 1

The eighteenth article of amendment to the Constitution of the United States is hereby repealed.

Section 2

The transportation or importation into any State, Territory, or Possession of the United States for delivery or use therein of intoxicating liquors, in violation of the laws thereof, is hereby prohibited.

Section 3

The article shall be inoperative unless it shall have been ratified as an amendment to the Constitution by conventions in the several States, as provided in the Constitution, within seven years from the date of the submission hereof to the States by the Congress.

Ratified 12/5/1933

Amendment 22 – Presidential Term Limits

Section 1

No person shall be elected to the office of the President more than twice, and no person who has held the office of President, or acted as President, for more than two years of a term to which some other person was elected President shall be elected to the office of the President more than once. But this Article shall not apply to any person holding the office of President, when this Article was proposed by the Congress, and shall not prevent any person who may be holding the office of President, or acting as President, during the term within which this Article becomes operative from holding the office of President or acting as President during the remainder of such term.

Section 2

This article shall be inoperative unless it shall have been ratified as an amendment to the Constitution by the legislatures of three-fourths of the several States within seven years from the date of its submission to the States by the Congress.

Ratified 2/27/1951

Amendment 23 – Presidential Vote for District of Columbia

Section 1

The District constituting the seat of Government of the United States shall appoint in such manner as the Congress may direct: A number of electors of President and Vice President equal to the whole number of Senators and Representatives in Congress to which the District would be entitled if it were a State, but in no event more than the least populous State; they shall be in addition to those appointed by the States, but they shall be considered, for the purposes of the election of President and Vice President, to be electors appointed by a State; and they shall meet in the District and perform such duties as provided by the twelfth article of amendment.

Section 2

The Congress shall have power to enforce this article by appropriate legislation.

Ratified 3/29/1961

Amendment 24 – Poll Tax Barred

Section 1

The right of citizens of the United States to vote in any primary or other election for President or Vice President, for electors for President or Vice President, or for Senator or Representative in Congress, shall not be denied or abridged by the United States or any State by reason of failure to pay any poll tax or other tax.

Section 2

The Congress shall have power to enforce this article by appropriate legislation.

Ratified 1/23/1964

Amendment 25 – Presidential Disability and Succession

Section 1

In case of the removal of the President from office or of his death or resignation, the Vice President shall become President.

Section 2

Whenever there is a vacancy in the office of the Vice President, the President shall nominate a Vice President who shall take office upon confirmation by a majority vote of both Houses of Congress.

Section 3

Whenever the President transmits to the President pro tempore of the Senate and the Speaker of the House of Representatives his written declaration that he is unable to discharge the powers and duties of his office, and until he transmits to them a written declaration to the contrary, such powers and duties shall be discharged by the Vice President as Acting President.

Section 4

Whenever the Vice President and a majority of either the principal officers of the executive departments or of such other body as Congress may by law provide, transmit to the President pro tempore of the Senate and the Speaker of the House of Representatives their written declaration that the President is unable to discharge the powers and duties of his office, the Vice President shall immediately assume the powers and duties of the office as Acting President.

Thereafter, when the President transmits to the President pro tempore of the Senate and the Speaker of the House of Representatives his written declaration that no inability exists, he shall resume the powers and duties of his office unless the Vice President and a majority of either the principal officers of the executive department or of such other body as Congress may by law provide, transmit within four days to the President pro tempore of the Senate and the Speaker of the House of Representatives their written declaration that the President is unable to discharge the powers and duties of his office. Thereupon Congress shall decide the issue, assembling within forty eight hours for that purpose if not in session. If the Congress, within twenty one days after receipt of the latter written declaration, or, if Congress is not in session, within twenty one days after Congress is required to assemble, determines by two thirds vote of both Houses that the President is unable to discharge the powers and duties of his office, the Vice President shall continue to discharge the same as Acting President; otherwise, the President shall resume the powers and duties of his office. **Ratified 2/10/1967**

Amendment 26 – Voting Age Set to 18 Years

Section 1

The right of citizens of the United States, who are eighteen years of age or older, to vote shall not be denied or abridged by the United States or by any State on account of age.

Section 2

The Congress shall have power to enforce this article by appropriate legislation.

Ratified 7/1/1971

Amendment 27 – Limiting Congressional Pay Increases

No law, varying the compensation for the services of the Senators and Representatives, shall take effect, until an election of Representatives shall have intervened.

Ratified 5/7/1992

As the review of the United States Constitution concludes, let us see what some historians have said about three important issues that stand out as key factors that make this a timeless and priceless document concerning the form and function of government.

The Federal Government and State Rights

For much of American history, the balance between governmental authority and individual liberty was understood and accepted. Federal power was confined to that which was specifically enumerated in the Constitution and no more. And that power was further limited, for it was dispersed among three Federal branches—the legislative, executive, and judicial. Beyond that, the power remained with the states and ultimately the people.[15]

Checks and Balances and Separation of Powers

The Constitution creates three branches of government of equal 'rank' in relation to each other. No branch is higher or lower than any other, and no branch controls the others; each has independent authority and unique powers.[16]

Without an adequate check on the legislative and executive branches, the government could act arbitrarily and strip citizens of their constitutional rights.[17]

The separation of powers and checks and balances are two fundamental principles underlying the Constitution. They work together to present a tyrannous concentration of power in any one branch, to check and restrain Government, and, ultimately, to protect the rights and liberties of citizens.[18]

Bill of Rights

What makes the Bill of Rights an effective check on the other two branches of government is the recognition of the "paramount" role of the constitution.[19]

The Bill of Rights is a distinctive and impressive mark of our liberty. Unlike the citizens of many other countries, Americans are protected from their government in the exercise of fundamental equal rights.[20]

The Story Continues

The first three words of the United States Constitution are "We the people."

Those simple words give all Americans the right and the responsibility to take ownership of our problems and take leadership in the task to fix those same problems. These words also give us hope in our task to stand firm in our freedom because we are not alone in this endeavor. Our military force keeps America free. These men and women have volunteered to stand watch for many reasons, but one stands tall—their love of liberty. There is also a great army of citizen soldiers in every corner of this land who may not be in uniform but are just as passionate about liberty. "We the people" can win many battles in our fight to maintain our freedom, but we still need help to win the war. We must fight because of the sacrifice our forefathers and family members made. We must fight so we can be free today. Most importantly, we must fight so future generations of Americans can enjoy the precious gift of freedom that is only found in America.

For Americans who are Christ followers, standing firm in freedom demands that we add three words to the phrase "We the people." This is not a formal request to change the Constitution, but these words will make a vital impact in the hearts and minds of Christ followers as we strive to win the war of maintaining our liberty in America. The revised phase is "We the people as Christ followers." In addition to our responsibilities as "We the people," Christ followers have additional tasks that involve calling upon the power of God and his Word to join us in this fight. In recent years Christians have been guilty of apathy and neglect in keeping Christian principles and morality in every aspect of our society. Christ followers are responsible for allowing this great nation to be considered by some as no longer a Christian nation. As America travels at supersonic speed away from the truth of the Word of God, it is reasonable to question whether or not America is still a Christian nation. Now is the time for Christian Americans to act. The way to move forward is to go back to our founding principles and fulfill our biblical responsibilities as followers of Jesus Christ.

The final two chapters combine to give ten actions steps that Americans and Christ following Americans need to take in order to help return the United States of America to its former glory. These ten steps may not be a comprehensive list of actions that must be taken in order to stand firm in our freedom, but it should be an effective starting point to guide America back to its founding principles. President Ronald Reagan kept a quote on his desk in the Oval Office that said, "IT CAN BE DONE." In the spirit of President Reagan, this can be done.

CHAPTER 7
How to Stand Firm in Freedom as "We the People"

Being born and raised in America, I have no experience with what it is like to live in other countries or be ruled by other forms of government. My exposure to other countries has been limited to occasional trips to Europe and South America. Friends and family who have traveled more extensively affirm my suspicions: Americans are truly blessed to live in America. Our liberty is unparalleled. The opportunity for success and happiness that results from our freedom is unmatched anywhere in the world. This belief doesn't make Americans better than the billions of other people who are scattered all around the world, but it does, make us exceptional. We enjoy, and in too many cases we take for granted, the freedoms that citizens of other nations cannot even imagine.

For the above reasons and more, we should be thankful for all of the former generations of Americans who have made this possible. In addition, American Christ followers should be thankful to God for our freedom. In the times that we find ourselves, Americans should also be determined to take the necessary steps in response to our current national strife and be willing to be proactive in preventing a return to a declining nation that is a result of a departure from our founding principles. Please make these five suggestions part of your plan to stand firm in your freedom as "We the people."

Stand Firm against Political Correctness

Political correctness has become the latest weapon of choice to shut down the free and legitimate practice of the First Amendment. This is a clever trick. Political correctness has found its way into almost every conversation and corner of American society. What is political correctness? It is a desire not to offend a people group, through words or actions, that might be perceived as disadvantaged, discriminated against, or just different. People will now preface any questionable comments by saying, "I want to be politically correct." The fear of offense, in most cases, will automatically limit or censor the content of any conversation. Some of the subjects that have become prime targets of this free-speech-killing movement are politics, religion, race, and the practice of any immoral or unusual behavior.

The impact of the political correctness movement on each American's freedom has been significant. The self-proclaimed victims cry, "Unfair!" and easily silence the rights of those who have the right to speak against them or their cause, inside the rule of law. The result is self-censorship of an individual's First Amendment right of free speech. Do you see how it works? An opponent can silence an enemy by shouting, "That's not politically correct!" It is simple and effective.

American society, from its founding, has practiced free speech. Political correctness is anti-free speech. If Americans give up their free speech rights, other freedoms cannot be far behind. If Christ followers in America give up their free speech rights because of political correctness, their message of forgiveness in Jesus Christ may cease being shared. The message of salvation in Jesus Christ alone is by definition offensive. A politically correct world would not allow an offensive message to be communicated, especially one that speaks of people going to hell because of their lack of belief in the fact that God raised Jesus Christ from the dead. This could silence the church and bring a serious decline in the number of Christ followers. Sadly, this is already happening. Even the message of this book would be silenced. To claim that God may choose to help one religion over another is not being politically correct. In addition, to say that a strict adherence to America's founding documents would help return America back to its former glory would also be unacceptable. The damaging practice of political correctness that has infected American culture must be stopped. We must not be intimidated by these two poisonous words. We must be civil in our discourse, but we cannot allow our free speech to be silenced any longer. We must continue to engage people with diverse thoughts and opinions, debate them, and be willing to convince them of our beliefs. This is a vital part of what it means to be American. Stand firm against political correctness.

Stand Firm for Religious Liberty

Religious liberty is described in the first section of the First Amendment of the United States Constitution. Matthew Spalding states, "Religious liberty, and the proper understanding of the relationship of religion and politics, is a key principle of liberty."[1] Religious liberty is not just an issue that Christ followers or other religious groups should be interested in preserving. Maintaining our religious liberty should be a concern for all Americans. Many American citizens and the courts have completely distorted the original meaning of the "establishment clause" of the First Amendment, which states, "Congress shall make no law respecting an establishment of religion, or prohibiting the free exercise thereof; . . . " How this distortion happened can be a blueprint for how other liberties in the Constitution could be changed, and we need to be on guard against this type of deception.

The United States Supreme Court and the anti-Christian movement in America have succeeded in convincing many Americans to give up the practice of their faith outside their individual houses of worship. People who want to pray at a public gathering or display a monument of the Ten Commandments are treated like criminals. It is now common practice to accept that any reference to God is not allowed in the public square. The tactic of these groups has been to spread the lie that there are words in the First Amendment that are not really there. What are these added words? This non-existent phrase is "separation of church and state."

This story can be succinctly told with a few quotes from several expert historians. Gerard Bradley states, "The First Amendment put the churches on an equal footing: No establishment of religion is constitutionally permissible at the federal level."[2] Bradley continues, "Promoting religion was a proper governmental action because affirming the existence of God and supporting religion promotes the common good."[3] Bradley further states, "Government's purpose was to protect the right to practice one's faith as long as doing so did not violate the rights of others or the requirements of the common good."[4] Bradley finally says, "In fact, the First Amendment does not say anything about a wall of separation. That phrase comes from a letter that Thomas Jefferson wrote 13 years after the First Amendment was written and ratified by the people."[5] Mark Levin affirms Bradley's belief and says, "There is simply no historical foundation for the proposition that the framers intended to build a 'wall of separation' that was constitutionalized in Everson."[6] Everson vs. Board of Education was a 1947

Supreme Court case that changed the balance between government and religion. Levin continues this discussion in his book *Men in Black* and says, "For the last several decades, the Court, based on a misreading of Thomas Jefferson's now famous letter to the Danbury Baptists, has seized on the mistaken idea that the Constitution requires a severe 'wall of separation' between church and state."[7] Levin continues with this bold statement, "But there is one conclusion we can draw: The Supreme Court has simply abolished your right to the free exercise of your religion in public."[8]

Christians need to take back the true meaning of the first sixteen words of the First Amendment and stand firm in religious liberty. The brave men and women who battled the seas, sickness, and the harsh environment of the New World came to America to practice their religion without interference. We must continue their bravery. Dr. Ben Carson states in his book, *America the Beautiful*, that, "There is nothing at all in our founding documents forbidding or denigrating religious expression in public life."[9] Educate yourself, be bold, and stand firm for religious liberty.

Stand Firm in American History

There are two easy steps in standing firm in American history. It is as simple as going back to school. First, be a student of American history. You may be asking yourself, "How do I become a student of American history?" A simple first step can be to use the content of this book. This book includes complete copies of the Declaration of Independence, the United States Constitution, the Pledge of Allegiance, the national anthem, and the citizenship oath. Other significant events of early American history are also included in *The Liberty Keys*. You can expand your knowledge of these events by studying those topics you find interesting. In addition, this book includes a list of recourses used for the research of the topics included. Please use *The Liberty Keys* as start in your journey as a student of American history. Once you find a trusted writer—I hope that I am one of them—use their references as source material for your study. Make sure that the resources you read are historically reliable. Too many writers put into their writing historical or political bias that attempts to rewrite American history. Carefully verify all of your reading material before trusting it. I believe that if every American had a better understanding of the true story of America's founding, there would be a greater desire to maintain the founders' vision for America.

Do more than just read. Visit the historic sites where these events took place. Instead of going to the beach or a theme park, go to Boston, New York, or Philadelphia. Study the locations of our founders' defeats and victories before you arrive so you will be better prepared to learn in greater depth the real history of our founding. Smell the air, taste the food, and see what the founders saw in order to get the best understanding of our history.

The second step in standing firm in American history is being a teacher of our history. You don't have to wait until you know everything to become a teacher. Tell others what you learned today about our history. If you have a favorite founding father, like George Washington, tell your friends about a trip to Mount Vernon or volunteer to tell a school, community, or church group about your trip. As you teach, don't be afraid to be excited about our history. Thomas Jefferson said that America's freedom depended upon an educated citizenry. Teach our history and be part of keeping America free. Teach others the importance of participating in the electoral process. Teach your family about how a bill starts in Congress and then the steps required to reach the desk of the President.

There are countless subjects to study and teach about America. Enjoy getting to know America and tell others about it. Stand firm in America history.

Stand Firm for American Restoration

What is American restoration? It is not going back to a time in American history when everything was perfect and peaceful. I'm not sure that time has ever existed. It is not going back to a time when most citizens were patriotic and desired America to be strong. It is also not going back to a time when everyone wanted to live under the rule of law and admired our founding documents. American restoration is gaining back a sense of pride in what it means to be an American. It is a pride in our founding and the people and documents that make America an exceptional nation. It is being a patriot. It is a love to fly the flag and defend our freedom no matter the cost.

Although many of these sentiments exist today, there is an ongoing attack against this way of life. American restoration is a call to reestablish our greatness from the inside out. It is time to put passion for America into action. This is a fight for America's survival. There are four primary places that we must stop retreating and fight.

Take the Fight into the Classroom

On June 25, 1962, the United States Supreme Court banned prayer in public schools. Prior to that day and ever since, the classroom in America has been a battleground. The fight involves more than a child's struggle in learning how to solve a difficult math assignment; it is much more sinister. The battle is over politics, religion, and a balanced and accurate teaching of history, more specifically, American history. The battle is a full-frontal assault against America. The founding fathers believed that public education had benefits beyond educating children. Matthew Spalding states in his book, *We Still Hold These Truths*, "Education was the mechanism for the general diffusion of knowledge, and the Founders believed that widespread popular education was the ultimate check on tyranny."[10] What the founders did not anticipate was that politicians, school administrators, and teachers scattered across America are now teaching the benefits of government tyranny. Teachers replaced lessons concerning the value of freedom with ones promoting the value of government protection and assistance. This is not a new fight; generations of children have already been infected by this misinformation and we are seeing the results before us in living color. The major crisis of radical liberalism in our colleges and universities is directly attributed to the training that students received in their elementary and secondary school experience. The former students are now the professors and parents of the current students who have not received accurate information concerning America's founding and the benefits of liberty.

What can we do to win this fight? It requires divine intervention, but as we watch and wait for God to act, there are many steps we can take. The actions we can take are some of the very ones that are already being taken. Parents can take a greater role in shaping the public schools by becoming active in parent organizations, running for local school board posts, or even becoming teachers and administrators. Being on the inside is a great tactical position for change.

Another option is home schooling. Home schooling can give parents an even greater opportunity to instill personal and or religious values into their children as well as preparing them for life or additional education. If home schooling is not a realistic possibility, private schools maybe an option. We will lose the classroom if we give up the fight and surrender.

Take the Fight into the Courthouse

Before you jump to any conclusions, this is not a call to fill the courts with countless and frivolous lawsuits. Lawyers and judges have been attacking what is great about America for centuries through the legal system. It is time, however, to reverse course. This is a simple fight with just a few recommendations: become a lawyer, a law professor, a judge, or take legal action, if absolutely necessary, to stand up against the attacks against our rule of law. It's time for the people who desire to preserve America as founded and hold an originalist view of interpreting the United States Constitution to save America from the progressive movement. An originalist believes that the United States Constitution should be interpreted as the founders intended it to be interpreted. Progressives believe that the Constitution is a "living and breathing" document. They are convinced that the Constitution should be changed as American society evolves. They also believe that the Founders wrote a document with too many limitations on the government's power. Courthouses across the land need an army of originalists to uphold our founding principles. Stand firm in the courthouse.

Take the Fight to All Levels of Government

This fight will be ugly, so I will keep my words brief. America needs a new breed of politician. There may be some out there, but they are getting harder to find. America needs statesmen and stateswomen who are willing to put America above personal interest. We don't need selfish career politicians whose only desires are for fame and fortune. We need selfless men and women who have common sense instead of inflated egos and greed for money and power. Their service needs to be limited. They need to fix the problems, mentor others, and get out. This may sound like an impossible task, but it can be accomplished. Start running for office; America needs you.

America also needs a new breed of citizen, a citizen who is willing to participate in politics by voting. I know that there are millions of voters already faithfully casting their votes, but America needs more participation in the election process. Elections are often won or lost by narrow margins. Voting is not only a hard-fought privilege, it is necessary for our freedom to continue. The opposition party may have these same goals, but our desire to save America can't just be a dream. It requires votes! Learn all you can about the candidates and issues, and then vote. Vote to clean out the old and entrenched politicians. Support and vote for candidates who will honor our founding documents. Vote to erase tyranny and expand our freedom. Vote! Please vote!

Take the Fight into the Economy

One of the biggest targets in the crosshairs of the enemies of America's founding and the pursuit of happiness is the United States economy. Free market capitalism has proven itself to be the engine that drives the greatest economy in history. You don't have to be an economist to know that capitalism has been given a bad reputation because of horror stories that have been told about its brutality. Yes, fortunes are easily made and lost. Yes, the risks can be high, but the payoff can also be high. Proponents of big government say that our economy is unfair and the government needs to level the playing field. I strongly disagree. We must protect our economy. We must continue with what works.

There are many action steps people can take to fight for our economy, but here are three basic steps. I compare these recommendations to PT or physical training in the military. PT gets soldiers in peak physical condition so they can fight. My suggestions are FT, or fiscal training. FT will get citizens in financial shape in order to stand firm in our economy. These suggestions are in no way based upon any economic expertise—just common sense and personal experience. There may be legitimate or lame excuses for not wanting to try these three simple suggestions. All three can be done simultaneously or one at a time. Give them a try. First, only spend what you can afford based upon your income. Most Americans want to have the "stuff" everyone else has or more. Prepare a budget and live by it. Second, pay off your debt. Debt puts shackles on people. Debt can take away your freedom to enjoy your life. Dave Ramsey and other financial experts have great programs that can help you pay off your debt. Finally, save your money. You can determine how much money you need to save or you can also seek advice from an expert. I suggest that you save as much as you can afford. It is wise to be prepared for unforeseen expenses or to fulfill your dreams. These simple suggestions can also apply to the United States government. Stand firm for American restoration.

Stand Firm in the Rule of Law

America was designed to be a civil society and to function under the rule of law, which includes two simple principles. First, laws at the local, state, and federal levels are written and approved by the proper legislative bodies and then signed into law. Second, citizens and guests of America are expected to keep those laws and live peacefully with everyone within our civil society. If the laws are broken, then appropriate action is taken to determine guilt or innocence. If the defendant is guilty, then the punishment will be administered. It should be the desire of all Americans to live under the rule of law while peacefully pursuing their dreams and aspirations.

Not everyone who resides within the borders of the United States wants to live according to our nation's desire for a civil society. Some people recklessly break the law. The courtrooms and jails that are filled to more than capacity prove this sad truth. Fighting to keep our society under the rule of law is critical for our survival as a nation and must be waged inside the rule of law. Yes, we must play by the rules. You may be saying, "No one else is playing by the rules, why should I?" That is the point; this fight must take place inside the rule of law. Do I have a specific plan? No! You will find one; I have faith in you. It will be a tedious process, so be patient and keep fighting. We must stand firm in the rule of law.

CHAPTER 8
How to Stand Firm in Freedom as "We the People, as Christ Followers"

I have been an American my entire life. I have been a Christ follower all but eight of those years. The liberty that Christ followers have is not the liberty to do as we please, but it is freedom to be obedient to God's Word and his will and receive his blessings in return. American Christ followers have had it easy. Since our founding we have been able to publicly practice our faith with little opposition. All of that is rapidly changing. Christianity is under attack in America. At the present time the attacks do not appear to be at the same level of intensity as our fellow Christ followers in other parts of the world, but it is coming. It is time for Christ Followers to stand firm in our freedom and fight against the efforts to silence us.

I strongly believe that American Christ followers do not have the luxury to be unconcerned or uninvolved any longer in the matters of America's freedom and future. Although our "kingdom is not of this world," we must set an example for others to follow as we demonstrate the biblical principles of being a good citizen as described in chapter 5. We must also bring the power of God into our fight to return America back to our founding principles. We must ask for and expect God's help. Please make these five suggestions part of your plan to stand firm in your freedom as "we the people, as Christ followers."

Stand Firm in the Word of God

The list of available Christian-themed books is almost unending. The number of topics covered in these books is just as numerous. Many of these books are written about the Bible to help explain its meaning. Christians are reading about the Bible but too often fail to read the Bible. This failure has created a famine in the land. The famine is a lack of God's blessings upon his people and their land because Christ followers are not rooted and grounded in the Word of God. There is only one way to end the famine: read and obey God's Word. The best way to read the Bible is slowly. Reading the Bible is not a race to see how many verses, chapters, or books can be read. Reading the Word of God requires careful study. Each word is important and requires a thoughtful review. Each word is God's Word. The best way to know and understand God is to spend time with him and listen to his voice. Followers of Christ must listen to God by reading his Word slowly. Remember this: "The best way to grow is to read it slow."

A Message to Pastors

A sermon, or what could be better described as a talk, was delivered by pastor of a "Coffee Shop" church that I visited on a September morning. A long series of high-energy praise songs were interrupted only by a powerful video that described all of the wonderful work this church was doing to impact its community. As the sermon began, the preacher described in great detail the reasons he was not prepared to speak that morning. He boldly stated that there were interruptions at home as well as at his other job that hindered his study. He made it sound like he was the only person in that crowded coffee shop who had to deal with interruptions.

The next part of the message addressed the greatness of the particular text he would be using in his talk: John 3:16. The preacher kept his gaze focused on his iPad as he made exaggerated hand gestures and even raised and lowered his voice to emphasize the importance of this iconic passage. Additionally, the preacher quoted other writers concerning their thoughts about this powerful passage. As the preacher hurried through the final part of his talk, he finally read the Scripture as he concluded his message.

Sadly, this story is repeated countless times every week in Christian churches all across America. Too many American pastors have traded the powerful Word of God for a patchwork of personal opinions filled with self-help advice that might have a hint of Scripture in it to satisfy the minimum requirements for "the talk" to be called a sermon. Christ-following pastors who are called by God to preach have a huge responsibility to preach the Word of God. People who follow Jesus Christ need to hear the truth that is the Word of God. Additionally, non-Christ followers need to hear and respond to the truth of God's Word. It is the only truth that gives the world any hope from the consequences of their sin. In order for American Christ followers to have the courage to visibly live their faith and the power to fight for the future of America, they need instructions from the wisdom and knowledge of God. Preachers, preach the Word of God. Preachers, stand firm in the Word of God.

A Message to Christ Followers

Christ followers who attend American churches must demand that preachers preach the Word of God. Followers of Jesus Christ must not accept excuses from anyone for the lack of emphasis placed upon the Word of God. Christ Followers also need to make the study of God's Word the highest priority in their spiritual journey. Christians need to spend less time reading about the Bible and more time reading and absorbing it into their very being. Christ follower, stand firm in the Word of God.

Stand Firm with Prayer

Christ followers in America need help to save America. It would appear that we underutilize one of our most powerful resources. We are virtually powerless without it. This resource is prayer. Prayer must be effective because non-Christ followers seem to fear it! Scores of opponents do not want followers of Jesus Christ to pray in public or, if the truth be told, in private. The Bible commands followers of Jesus Christ to pray. First Thessalonians 5:17 states "pray without ceasing." There appear to be both prayer fatigue and prayer fear among the people of faith. An example of this phenomenon is the issue of prayer in public schools. Christ followers know that prayer was removed from public schools and too many dutifully accept this fact and comply. Prayer may have been formally removed from our public schools, but prayer can only be removed from our schools if Christ followers stop praying. As long as there are followers of Christ in our public schools, prayer will remain. As long as there are Christian parents who have children who attend public schools, prayer will remain in schools.

What would explain this prayer fatigue and prayer fear? Perhaps some followers of Christ believe that God is tired of listening to them and is not concerned about the issue of prayers not being offered in public. God has promised that he will hear and answer our prayers if we pray according to his will. God's resources are limitless. God desires to open the "windows of heaven and pour out for you a blessing until it overflows" (Malachi 3:10).

God can provide solutions to seemingly impossible problems. Some complain that their prayers remain unanswered. The fact that prayers appear to go unanswered does not relate to God's inability to answer prayer but rather our lack of purity. We must be in a proper relationship with God through his forgiveness of our sin in Jesus Christ before he will consider our prayers. It is important to remember that God requires his children to be "clean" before he will answer their prayers. Being clean simply means being forgiven. Being forgiven has two levels of clean. First, before a person can get God's response he or she must have a personal relationship with him through Jesus Christ. God will not just answer anyone. Second, the believer must ask for forgiveness at the opening of each prayer so God will listen. Psalm 24:3–4 is a reference for this practice. "Who may ascend into the hill of the Lord? And who may stand in His holy place? He who has clean hands and a pure heart, Who has not lifted up his soul to falsehood And has not sworn deceitfully."

Some may disagree, but for prayer to be effective it needs to include some key elements. Our prayers must be addressed to God the Father (Matthew 6:9), and our words are communicated to the Father by the Holy Spirit (Romans 8:26). Finally, all Christ followers must pray in the name of Jesus Christ (John 14:13–14). The name of Jesus gives our prayers power. Remember this truth: God does not grant prayer requests based upon the individual believer's character or goodness but on the believer's relationship with himself through Jesus Christ.

As we pray to God, in the name of Jesus, Christ followers seek God's will, strength, and help in all manner of life situations. One of the blessings of following Christ is that we have access, through prayer, to God himself and his unlimited power. Although life brings to everyone a certain number of trials and tribulations, Christ followers are accustomed to asking and receiving answers to our prayers. Through answered prayer, we are eyewitnesses to the power of God. Our experiences give us peace in this earthly life and absolute confidence for the next.

Christ followers must make prayer a priority. If you do not pray, who will? Who can? Have you committed to pray without ceasing? God is waiting to hear from you. He wants to answer his people according to his perfect will. Time is precious for everyone, and effective prayer requires much time and effort. Look at the issue of prayer from this sobering perspective. Do you believe that the Word of God is the only truth? If so, then you must believe that the God of the Bible is the only true and living God. Christ followers are praying to the only true and living God. He is the only one who can hear our prayers and act. Christ followers must put their faith into practice and pray with boldness and urgency.

Following are some items that need your attention and consideration as you pray: forgiveness of sin, spiritual awakening in America, the restoration of America's founding principles, every elected official, members of the armed forces, law enforcement, firefighters and other emergency personnel, the safety of America in a dangerous world, and unity and peace in America. Pray that other Americans and citizens of the nations will become Christ followers through the work of God and other Christ followers, families in America will be preserved and protected, and that pastors and churches that follow Christ will be proactive and fearless in helping to transform people with the love of Christ.

In 1 Timothy 2:1–4 the apostle Paul gives us instructions concerning how Christ followers must pray as citizens of America. "First of all, then, I urge that entreaties and prayers, petitions and thanksgivings, be made on behalf of all men, for kings and all who are in authority, so that we may lead a tranquil and quiet life in all godliness and dignity. This is good and acceptable in the sight of God our Savior, who desires all men to be saved and to come to the knowledge of the truth." Have you prayed enough to make an impact? Stand firm with prayer.

Stand Firm as a Christ Follower

Jesus spoke to His followers about how they are to be bold and visible in the practice of their faith. In our fight to return America to our founding principles, as a Christ follower you must stop hiding; you must remove your carnal camouflage and fight. Jesus has given us some specific responsibilities as we visibly represent Him in the world. These powerful words are recorded in Matthew 5:13–15:

> You are the salt of the earth; but if the salt has become
> tasteless, how can it be made salty again? It is no longer
> good for anything, except to be thrown out and trampled
> under foot by men. You are the light of the world. A city
> set on a hill cannot be hidden; nor does anyone light a lamp
> and put it under a basket, but on the lampstand, and it gives
> light to all who are in the house. Let your light shine before
> men in such a way that they may see your good works, and
> glorify your Father who is in heaven.

In his first illustration Jesus states that Christ followers are to be the salt of the earth. In this context Jesus is referring to the function of salt that acts as a preservative. As the salt of the earth, Christ followers are to help permeate the world with the Word of God in order to preserve morality and prevent spiritual decay. Christ followers are to put God's Word inside themselves through study and obedience and demonstrate God's truth as they live their lives.

Jesus's second illustration describes Christ followers as the light of the world. What does that mean? Followers of Christ have the Holy Spirit of God and the Word of God inside them. As Christ followers we should live according to Scripture and let the light of truth shine through us to illumine a dark and sin-filled world. Jesus said that the light that is inside his followers must shine. Let your light shine and stand firm as a Christ follower.

Stand Firm by Seeing the Power of God

The Bible contains the long and powerful story of the nation of Israel. It begins with Abram in the book of Genesis. God promised to give Abram a son, and later the promise expanded to include land that was called the "promised land." That promise continued to expand with a name change to Abraham, which means "the father of many," and the promise that his descendants would be as numerous as the stars in the sky. As the story continued, the family grew to include Abraham's son and grandson: Isaac and Jacob. This family, under the watchful eye of Abraham's great-grandson Joseph, moved down to Egypt because of a famine. Joseph had been sold into slavery and was sent to Egypt. With God's blessings, Joseph ended up second in command of the entire nation of Egypt.

After about four hundred years in Egypt, this family had grown into a large nation within the country of Egypt. Because of their growing numbers, the Egyptians feared the Hebrews and forced them into slavery. The Hebrews cried out to God to deliver them from their bondage. At this point in the story God called upon a man named Moses. He was given the task of leading the people out of Egypt and into the promised land. Pharaoh, the king of Egypt, was not going to allow this to happen.

After God had unleashed the power of the ten plagues upon the people, livestock, and land of Egypt, Pharaoh finally agreed to let the Hebrew people leave Egypt. Soon after their release, Pharaoh regretted his decision and chased after them. After Pharaoh had trapped his former slaves, the Hebrews, up against the Red Sea, he thought he had them right where he wanted them. God had promised Moses that He would deliver the sons of Israel from the land of Egypt. Keeping his promise, God delivered his people with a spectacular miracle. God divided the Red Sea and the people of God, led by Moses, crossed over on dry ground, escaping the Egyptians. As soon as all of the sons of Israel made it safely to the other side of the Red Sea, God brought the water back together on top of Pharaoh's army, killing everyone.

God then gave Moses the law and instructed him to send twelve men as spies into the promised land before the people would enter it. After the people heard the report from the spies concerning the land and those who inhabited it, they refused to enter into it because of their fear and lack of faith. Because of their lack of faith, God caused the Hebrew nation to wander in the wilderness for forty years until the generation of doubters died. Even the great leader Moses was forbidden to enter into the promised land because of his disobedience to God.

After Moses died, God chose Joshua to lead the people of God into the promised land. As recorded in the book of Joshua, God gave Joshua instructions to enter into the land by crossing the Jordan River. The first few chapters of the book of Joshua describe how God once again divided water in order for his people to cross over on dry land. God instructed

Joshua in chapter 4 to take up twelve stones from the middle of the Jordan and carry them to Gilgal. God also instructed Joshua to take up a second set of twelve stones that would be placed in the middle of the Jordan. Joshua 4:20–24 states:

> Those twelve stones which they had taken from the Jordan, Joshua set up at Gilgal. He said to the sons of Israel, "When your children ask their fathers in time to come, saying, 'What are these stones?' then you shall inform your children, saying, 'Israel crossed this Jordan on dry ground.' For the Lord your God dried up the waters of the Jordan before you until you had crossed, just as the Lord you God had done to the Red Sea, which He dried up before us until we had crossed; that all the peoples of the earth may know that the hand of the Lord is mighty, so that you may fear the Lord your God forever."

This powerful story can teach us a critical lesson. God wants to show all the peoples of the world, including every American, that he is indeed the only true and living God. One of the ways God does this is by visibly answering the prayers of his people. Sadly, some Christian Americans have joined the chorus of giving honor and legitimacy to the "gods" of other religions who are, according to the Bible, false. The silence of Christ followers in America has given non-believers a false understanding of the very nature of God. Exodus 20:2–6 records God's conversation with Moses as God describes himself. Listen to what God said in this familiar passage from the Ten Commandments.

> I am the Lord you God, who brought you out of the land of Egypt, out of the house of slavery. You shall have no other gods before Me. You shall

not make for yourself an idol, or any likeness of what is in heaven above or on the earth beneath or in the water under the earth. You shall not worship them or serve them; for I, the Lord your God, am a jealous God, visiting the iniquity of the fathers on the children, on the third and the fourth generations of those who hate Me, but showing lovingkindness to thousands, to those who love Me and keep My commandments.

When Christ-following Americans publicly call upon the only true and living God to solve the complicated problems we face as Americans, the entire world will see the power of God. Christian Americans have not allowed God's glory and power to be demonstrated because of our unwillingness to pray. I must admit that many of the nations of the world are not overly concerned about the future of America. For many of these nations, America is not the solution for the world's problems; America is the cause. I must also admit that America is not the solution God will use to save the world. God's plan is to save the peoples of the world from the penalty of their sin through the death and resurrection of Jesus Christ, but a healthy and strong America is an incredible platform God can use to draw millions of people into his kingdom. America must continue to live in liberty so that the people of the world will benefit from the faith practices of Christ followers and hear and see the power of God. Stand firm by seeing the power of God.

Stand Firm by Making Disciples of All the Nations

Christ followers have known since the moment Jesus instructed His disciples to "make disciples of all the nations" that telling others about the life changing power of Jesus Christ was their mandate. Below is the scripture passage known as the Great Commission.

And Jesus came up and spoke to them, saying, "All authority has been given to Me in heaven and on earth. Go therefore and make disciples of all the nations, baptizing them in the name of the Father and the Son and the Holy Spirit, teaching them to observe all that I commanded you; and lo, I am with you always, even to the end of the age." (Matthew 28:18–20)

Throughout Christian history there have been periods of great revival resulting in a sharp increase in the number of Christ followers. At other times there has been a turning away from the things of God and as a result a decline in the number of Christians in the world. Since Christians have been not sharing their faith in Jesus with the world, as instructed, there is a void that is being filled with other religions sharing their story of false hope and their "way" to heaven. Christ followers must never forget the words of Jesus found in John 14:6: "Jesus said to him, 'I am the way, and the truth, and the life; no one comes to the Father but through Me.'" Today, Christianity in America appears to be in a period of decline. Blame can be shared by all followers of Christ, but there are three significant reasons that explain this decline: population growth, political correctness, and immigration.

Population Growth

In many ways the decline in population of Christian Americans is all about the numbers. The birth rates of the population groups that are historically Christian have declined and have not kept pace with world-wide population growth. To compound the issue, the birth-rates of non-Christian population groups are significantly higher. For example, the growth rates of people groups that are primarily Hindu or Muslim have continued to increase. All signs point to a continuation of this trend that will only grow more significant in years to come. This stark reality makes it even more imperative that Christ followers every-where have a renewed since of urgency concerning making disciples. Every follower of Christ has been instructed by Jesus himself to make disciples. We must not only make disciples of our own children, but we must share Jesus Christ with the nations.

Political Correctness

The very nature of making disciples violates the principle of political correctness. Telling someone that if they do not ask God to forgive them of their sins by faith in Jesus Christ they will spend an eternity in a place called hell fits the definition of being politically incorrect. As mentioned above, political correctness takes on many forms and in many subtle and obvious ways is preaching the old doctrine of moral relativism. Moral relativism teaches that "Your path to heaven may be different than mine, but that does not make your path wrong." In short, political correctness can bully followers of Christ into silence and inaction regarding Jesus's command to make disciples of all the nations.

Too many Christian Americans are living under a self-imposed ban on personal evangelism. We are afraid to judge, confront, or challenge people concerning their personal faith beliefs. To make the situation even worse, political correctness in partnership with the universal fear of Muslim extremism has silenced additional Christ followers. We must never stop telling the world about the life-changing power of Jesus Christ. Not only is Jesus's Great Commission still in effect, the people of the world still need to hear and be transformed by the love of God as demonstrated in Jesus Christ.

Immigration

When the world comes to America bringing with them their culture and religion, we have a long history of welcoming them with opened arms. Historically, most of these arrivals desired to be Americans while also keeping their passion for their home countries. Today, however, it appears that many immigrants do not want to adopt American culture. Some new citizens and illegal immigrants are basically setting up satellite countries within the borders of America. Because of this reality, individual followers of Christ and churches must adopt the mindset of missionaries to share the message of Jesus Christ. As Christ followers we must change our mindset of isolationism and tell the world that is coming to America about Jesus Christ.

Christians must re-learn the old methods of evangelism and create new ones using the internet and social media to tell others about the life-changing power of Jesus Christ. Our goal is not to build a nation, but the kingdom of God. Only when the hearts of people change through the transformative power of Jesus will societies and nations change. We need to be bold and tireless in our efforts to challenge all forces trying to stop us when we share of the message of salvation through Jesus Christ with the people of the world. Stand firm by making disciples of all the nations.

The Story Continues

I want you to join me on my third trip to Mount Vernon. It appears that not much has changed since my last trip. The grounds are still immaculate. The trees have grown much taller and some must have died and been removed. The flowers arranged in the gardens look a little different but are still vibrant with color. The view of the Potomac from the rear of the house is still breathtaking. The main house was still white with a red roof that was glistening in the hot sun of this humid summer day. My fellow tourists were trying to find relief from the heat in the shade as they walked the grounds of the well-preserved estate of America's first president. Visitors, some winded and worn out from their hike around these historic and sacred grounds, were eagerly waiting to enter the mansion.

As I entered the central passage, I was impatiently waiting my turn to stand where this *Liberty Keys* adventure had started for me. As I took my turn in front of the framed key to the Bastille's main door that General Lafayette had given President Washington, I thought back to my previous trips and my thoughts concerning America's liberty. I also thought about where America was today in our struggle to maintain our freedom.

I must confess, this trip to Mount Vernon is an imaginary one, ten years into the future. In ten years, I am hopeful that America will be stronger and more prosperous than ever. I hope that our government and my fellow citizens will coexist in peace. In a decade, we will have survived several election cycles. I'm sure Congress will be dealing will some of the same issues unaddressed or ignored ten years earlier. I believe America's condition will be reflective of our efforts. If we follow the suggestions presented in this book, I believe America will be healthy and strong. I believe our future will be bright and full of hope. If we remain indifferent and uninvolved in America's present situation, our future will be uncertain and bleak. What future do you want for America?

I have faith in America's design. If we are wise and keep our trust in the founders' wisdom, the United States Constitution, we can remain strong indefinitely. I also have faith in Americans. We must live each day with a visible pride in American values and be model citizens willing to live and work within the rule of law. Historically, Americans have been willing to rise to the occasion when we find ourselves in a crisis. I also believe in our ability to be proactive and avoid many of the problems we have today by remaining alert and active in our liberty. Most importantly, as a Christ follower, I have faith in God to lead and protect us as we call upon him. Having read biblical prophecy, I have a good understanding of how the world will end. I know America is not the savior of the world—Jesus is—but a strong and healthy America makes the world a safer place, and America is the best platform from which Christ followers can reach a hurting world with the message of grace and peace only available in Jesus Christ.

I want to end this part of the story with a simple prayer. "Dear Heavenly Father, Thank you for the blessings of our history and our hopeful future as Americans. Thank you for our Founders and countless other Americans who have paid a heavy price for our freedom. I pray that we will be obedient stewards of Your bounty and that we will stand firm in our precious freedom all the days of our lives. May You continue to bless America. In the name of Jesus Christ, Amen."

RESOURCES

Herman Belz, *Constitutionalism and The Rule of Law in America* (Washington D.C.: The Heritage Foundation, 2009).

Gerard Bradley, *Religious Liberty in the American Republic* (Washington D.C.: The Heritage Foundation, 2008).

Ben Carson, *America the Beautiful* (Grand Rapids, MI: Zondervan, 2012).

Susan Dunn, *Sister Revolutions: French Lightning, American Light* (New York, NY: Faber and Faber, 1999).

James Gaines, *For Liberty and Glory: Washington, Lafayette, and Their Revolutions* (New York: W. W. Norton & Company, 2007).

Os Guinness, *A Free People's Suicide: Sustainable Freedom and The American Future* (Downers Grove, IL: IVP Books, 2012).

Christopher Hibbert, *The Days of the French Revolution* (New York: Harper Perennial, 1980).

Mark R. Levin, *Ameritopia* (New York, NY: Threshold Editions, 2012).

Mark R. Levin, *Liberty and Tyranny* (New York, NY: Threshold Editions, 2009).

Mark R. Levin, *Men in Black* (Washington D.C.: Regnery Publishing. 2005).

Matthew Spalding, *A Citizen's Introduction to the Declaration of Independence and the Constitution* (Washington D.C.: The Heritage Foundation, 2010).

Matthew Spalding, *We Still Hold These Truths: Rediscovering Our Principles, Reclaiming Our Future* (Wilmington, DE: ISI Books, 2009).

"To George Washington from Thomas Paine, 1 May 1790," *Founders Online, National Archives* (http://founders.archives.gov/documents/Washington/05-05-02-0238 [last update: 2015-02-20]). Source: *The Papers of George Washington, Presidential Series*, vol. 5, 16 January 1790–30 June 1790, ed. Dorothy Twohig, Mark A. Mastromarino, and Jack D. Warren. Charlottesville: University Press of Virginia, 1996, 369–70.

U.S. Government Printing Office, *Our American Government, 2003 Edition* (Washington D.C.: U.S. Government Printing Office, 2003).

NOTES

Foreword

1. James Gaines, *For Liberty and Glory: Washington, Lafayette, and Their Revolutions*
(New York: W. W. Norton & Company, 2007), 330.
2. "To George Washington from Thomas Paine, 1 May 1790," Founders Online, National Archives, http://founders.archives.gov/documents/Washington/05-05-02-0238 (last updated: 2015-02-20).

1. Freedom Desired

1. Matthew Spalding, *A Citizen's Introduction to the Declaration of Independence and The Constitution* (Washington D.C.: The Heritage Foundation, 2010), 3.
2. James Gaines, *For Liberty and Glory: Washington, Lafayette, and Their Revolutions*
(New York: W. W. Norton & Company, 2007), 164.
3. Susan Dunn, *Sister Revolutions: French Lightning, American Light*
(New York: Faber and Faber, Inc., 1999), 27.
4. Ibid, 28.
5. Ibid, 59.
6. Ibid, 74.

2. Freedom Declared

1. Dunn, *Sister Revolutions* 36

2. Ibid, 91.

3. Ibid, 69.

4. Freedom's Demise

1. Gaines, *For Liberty and Glory*166.

2. Dunn, *Sister Revolutions*, 24.

3. Ibid, 63.

4. Os Guinness, *A Free People's Suicide: Sustainable Freedom and The American Future*

(Downers Grove, IL: IVP Books, 2012), 19.

5. Dunn, *Sister Revolutions*, 201.

6. Guinness, *A Free People's Suicide*, 57.

7. Ibid, 18.

8. Ibid, 166.

9. Dunn, *Sister Revolutions*, 201.

10. Mark R. Levin, *Men in Black* (Washington D.C.: Regnery Publishing. 2005), ix.

11. Guinness, *A Free People's Suicide* 191.

5. Freedom's Design—The Biblical Model

1. Herman Belz, *Constitutionalism and The Rule of Law in America* (Washington D.C.: The Heritage Foundation, 2009), vii.

6. Freedom's Design—The American Model

1. Matthew Spalding, *We Still Hold These Truths: Rediscovering Our Principles,*

Reclaiming Our Future (Wilmington, DE: ISI Books, 2009), 118.

2. Ibid.

3. Dunn, *Sister Revolutions*, 30.

4. Gerard Bradley, *Religious Liberty in the American Republic* (Washington D.C.: The Heritage Foundation, 2008), 24.

5. Ibid.

6. Mark R. Levin, *Liberty and Tyranny* (New York, NY: Threshold Editions, 2009), 38.

7. Spalding, *We Still Hold These Truths*, 100.

8. Ibid, 8.

9. Ibid, 98.

10. Belz, *Constitutionalism and The Rule of Law in America*, 9.

11. Ben Carson, *America the Beautiful* (Grand Rapids, MI: Zondervan, 2012), 38.

12. Spalding, *We Still Hold These Truths*, 89.

13. Ibid, 93.

14. Gaines, *For Liberty and Glory*, 247.

15. Levin, *Liberty and Tyranny*, 5.

16. Spalding, *We Still Hold These Truths*, 101.

17. Dunn, *Sister Revolutions*, 148.

18. U.S. Government Printing Office, *Our American Government, 2003 Edition* (Washington D.C.: U.S. Government Printing Office, 2003), 5.

19. Dunn, *Sister Revolutions*, 147.

20. Spalding, *We Still Hold These Truths*, 111.

7. How to Stand Firm in Freedom as "We the People"

1. Spalding, *We Still Hold These Truths*, 52.

2. Bradley, *Religious Liberty in the American Republic*, 4.

3. Ibid, 9.

4. Ibid, 15.

5. Ibid, 39.

6. Levin, *Liberty and Tyranny*, 31.

7. Levin, *Men in Black*, 35.

8. Ibid.

9. Carson, *America the Beautiful*, 48.

10. Spalding, *We Still Hold These Truths*, 146.